COOK SLOW

COOK SLOW

90 SIMPLE, CHILLED-OUT, STRESS-FREE RECIPES FOR SLOW COOKERS & CONVENTIONAL OVENS

Dean Edwards

hamlyn

For Uncle Steve

An Hachette UK Company
www.hachette.co.uk

First published in Great Britain in 2018 by Hamlyn, an imprint of
Octopus Publishing Group Ltd
Carmelite House
50 Victoria Embankment
London EC4Y 0DZ
www.octopusbooks.co.uk

ISBN 978-1-784-72430-6

A CIP catalogue record for this book is available from the British
Library.

Printed and bound in China

10 9 8 7 6 5 4 3 2

Commissioning Editor: Sarah Reece
Senior Editor: Pollyanna Poulter
Copy Editor: Kristin Jensen
Senior Designer: Jaz Bahra
Photographer: Ria Osborne
Prop Stylist: Cynthia Blackett
Home Economist and Food Stylist: Sara Lewis
Production Manager: Caroline Alberti

Contents

Introduction →

At a time when society tells us that we should live our lives at a thousand miles an hour, why have I decided to take inspiration from a cooking process that totally goes against this train of thought? I'll tell you why: because cooking food slowly not only is the best method for transforming basic, inexpensive ingredients into something very special, but there is also a warm feeling that develops inside knowing that the work is done and the magic is happening in the pot or slow cooker. Whether you use this time to put your feet up, take a leisurely walk with your four-legged friends or spend some time with the little ones, the choice is yours. And then the big reveal comes – that steaming stew, curry or broth can be brought to the table and devoured by a hungry family or friends who no doubt have been salivating at the aromas coming from the kitchen. It's a win-win situation for everyone.

WHY I TURNED TO SLOW COOKING

I want to share with you two very specific moments that really stand out as shaping the direction that my life has taken. The first being in 2006 when I naively thought that entering a cooking competition called 'Masterchef' wouldn't change anything in my life. Wow, how wrong was I? Still to this day the hardest thing I've ever taken part in, but what an experience and I've been living the dream ever since. I still have to pinch myself because I know how lucky I am to be living out my passion of working with food every day. I will always be thankful for the opportunity the show gave me. The second moment my life changed was the day in 2009 when my daughter Indie was born. This little chick changed everything for me. My life is dedicated to her, she has shaped me into the man I am today and I'm introducing her here because the gushing father in me talks about her every other sentence so I wouldn't want you to be wondering who she is.

Now to make a small confession: I got kind of lost for a while. Everything that had previously led me to a career in food and cooking had fallen to one side. A combination of a busman's holiday and having a daughter had directed my focus on food to serving up something quick, simple and easy for our meals. Now I'm not saying that's a bad thing at all, but I didn't realize how far I had drifted away from everything that had made me fall in love with food and cooking in the first place. Thinking about it, I realized that I craved the days where I used to wake up and immediately start to plan my dinner, whether that was through the joy of opening up a cookbook and being inspired to try something new or trying to recreate

Sometimes the longer it cooks, the better

something I had eaten in a restaurant or on my travels. I had fallen into the trap of cooking only what my daughter enjoyed and not taking too many chances. Let's be honest – any parent will tell you the crushing feeling when you slave over a dinner for your little ones, only for them to turn round and turn their noses up at it. Why do I bother? seemed to be a question I found frequently popping into my head.

I decided to find again the relaxing fulfilment of not only the preparation and cooking, but also of the eating and the happiness that comes from feeding family and friends. We can achieve fulfilment through food in many different ways, be it organized, precise preparation or ease of process, let alone the reward of eating delicious, nourishing food as a result of your labours. There is a time and a place for all types of cooking and all types of cuisines, but it was the process of slow cooking that really got my creative juices flowing and reinvigorated my passion in a big way. Since the day I started to cook, it wasn't just the end result that I loved; it was the process, the chopping, stirring, simmering and tasting along the way that also added to the experience. Oh, and the perks, too, like sneakily devouring that first taste of the meat as it's being carved for Sunday lunch – funnily, this sliver of meat always tastes so much better than anything I'm going to go on to eat. You know what I'm talking about!

TRANSFORMING THE MOST MODEST OF INGREDIENTS

Food can do strange things to people – in a good way, of course. Growing up, if we were lucky enough to have steak, it was a huge treat. I loved steak, just as it was; golden with a crispy edge of fat running down its length was the stuff of dreams for a growing lad. Then my dad introduced me to a simple marinade of sliced garlic and Worcestershire sauce. We used to leave it overnight and I remember the anticipation killing me. Maybe that's why I fell in love with food – something as simple as a two-ingredient marinade can magically transform a dish you enjoy into a recipe you totally adore.

I'm not going to go all scientific on you, but at 70°C (160°F) something magical happens. At that temperature, the so-called tougher or chewier cuts of meat begin to break down and become meltingly tender and a joy to eat. Basic ingredients can blend into something spectacular. Something as simple as a beef stew using inexpensive ingredients can become a delicious hearty meal the whole family can enjoy. In recent years I have seen

several unusual cuts of meat as well as old favourites such as oxtail popping up in restaurants and butchers. These are traditionally cheaper cuts that require a little more love and attention, but they sure do pack a punch in the flavour department. The process of slow cooking is by no means confined to just meat dishes – vegetables form a huge part of the slow cooking process. Onions melt away, root vegetables become tender and sweet and the possibilities are endless. Fish and shellfish must not be forgotten either; by cooking the sauce or broth over a prolonged period of time then adding the fish at the last minute, you can create dishes that are both delicate but complex in flavour. The recipes in this book can be cooked over 1 hour, 2 hours or even 8 hours, whatever your time restraints allow. Sometimes the longer it cooks, the better. Just set the oven or slow cooker to low and allow those ingredients to cook slowly.

BUSY LIVES NEED FLEXIBLE MEALTIMES

Slow cookers are back with a bang, no longer seen as that piece of kitchen equipment that never gets used and takes pride of place in the back of the cupboard. And this sort of cooking suits all sorts, from professionals to families to students. Another reason I love

TIPS FOR SLOW COOKERS

1   Try not to peek. Some recipes will benefit from a quick stir, but every time you lift that lid, you will add minutes to your cooking time.
2   Don't overcrowd the pot. Try not to fill your slow cooker over halfway.
3   I've adjusted the recipes to give you the amount of liquid required for the recipes, but because liquids won't be able to reduce in the slow cooker, as a general rule of thumb you should reduce the amount of liquid required in the conventional method by around half. Alcohol, on the other hand, must be reduced *before* going in the slow cooker or only add a splash because a little goes a long way.
4   For some recipes you will need to bring water or stock to the boil *before* adding it to the slow cooker, or it will never get hot enough to cook the food.
5   As a general rule of thumb, it will take twice as long to cook a recipe on the low setting as the high setting. Be mindful that a lot of slow cooker recipes use ingredients that benefit from a slow cooking process, so try not to be tempted to cut corners.
6   When finishing recipes, dairy should be added towards the end of the cooking time, so stir through cream and yogurt just before serving.

the slow cooker and this way of cooking is that if need be, a family can eat at different times as the meal keeps ticking over. So if the kids are moaning that they are hungry after school, it's good to go, and if parents want to eat later and enjoy some peace and quiet with their meal, that's great too. The idea of eating as a family unit is a lovely one, but in reality it's not always possible because busy lifestyles can dictate that we all eat at different times.

HOW SLOW WILL YOU GO?

Don't own a slow cooker? Don't panic! All the recipes in this book can be cooked either conventionally in the oven or in your slow cooker, so whichever way you decide to go, both bases are covered. What you're getting here is a two-for-one bonus – twice as much work for me in testing these recipes to make it twice as easy for you!

In addition to tasty, heart-warming recipes that you can serve up to your family and friends, be it from a few store cupboard ingredients or trying an exciting new ingredient or a familiar ingredient in a new way, you will also find some really useful tips scattered throughout this book and even some time-saving techniques, should you need them.

My ethos on food is simple. There are no fad diets or crazes, I simply cook and eat what I enjoy and use ingredients that are readily available and easily accessible but always with a mind on using the best-quality produce that I can lay my hands on. It's a cliché but I love to cook and I think that love comes through in the food. Feed the body and nourish the soul.

TRICKS TO GET AHEAD

If I have a busy day ahead of me, I prep my meals the evening before, then before I head out the door in the morning, I just dump the ingredients into my slow cooker, switch on the heat and away I go.

You do need to get organized when you have a little more time on your hands, so making an allowance for knocking up a batch of Time Saver Onions, Garlic Base or Curry Base (see pages 14–15 and keep an eye out for the clock icon) will make life easier in the long run. Planning your meals will not only save you time, but by shopping this way it will be easier on your pocket too.

All the recipes can be cooked in the oven or in your slow cooker

TIME SAVER RECIPES 🕐

Many great recipes rely on the cook layering the flavours within the dish. For me, the base of many classics is beautifully sweet, sticky and golden onions. Sure, you could just pop a raw sliced onion into your slow cooker, but by preparing ahead and having these time savers in the freezer, you can throw them straight in – no messing, no faffing, just bags of flavour added into your recipe with minimum effort. These three versions will ensure your meal prep will be quick and easy. The clock icon (as shown above) has been included in every recipe where you can use these time saver recipes.

TIME SAVER ONIONS

MAKES 6 PORTIONS

8 large onions, approx. 1 kg
    (2 lb 4 oz)
4 tablespoons oil
50 g (1¾ oz) unsalted butter
salt and pepper
6 small freezer bags

TIME SAVER GARLIC BASE

MAKES 6 PORTIONS

8 large onions, approx. 1 kg
    (2 lb 4 oz)
4 tablespoons oil
50 g (1¾ oz) unsalted butter
1 head of garlic, crushed
6 small freezer bags

TIME SAVER CURRY BASE

MAKES 6 PORTIONS

8 large onions, approx. 1 kg
    (2 lb 4 oz)
4 tablespoons oil
50 g (1¾ oz) unsalted butter
1 head of garlic, crushed
200 g (7 oz) fresh root ginger,
    grated
6 small freezer bags

CONVENTIONAL METHOD

1 Peel and finely slice or dice your onions. Add the oil and butter to a large pan set over a low to medium heat, then add the onions and season with salt and pepper. Cook for 20–25 minutes, stirring frequently. This may seem like a long time, but for this amount of onions, you will need it. The onions will go a beautiful golden colour. If making the Garlic Base or Curry Base, add the additional ingredients at this stage and cook for a further 2–3 minutes.
2 Portion into labelled freezer bags, then leave to cool. Pop into the freezer and use within 3 months.

SLOW COOKER METHOD

1 Place all the ingredients in your slow cooker along with a good pinch of salt and pepper. Stir well, then pop on the lid and cook on the low setting for 8 hours.

TIP

To use the time saver recipes straight from frozen, run the ziplock bag under a hot tap for a few seconds before tipping into your slow cooker.

Family Favourites

This chapter showcases dishes to be served up when I have family coming over for dinner and there are some stunners in here. Indie loves the Sticky Cherry Cola Baby Back Ribs. Cooking the ribs slowly means the meat is beautifully tender and falling off the bone. This is a dream combination alongside the Three Cheese Mac with Chorizo Crumb.

Spending time around the family dinner table seems to be something we are rapidly forgetting how to do. I find that making the effort to put a meal on the table that the whole family will enjoy inspires that time together. Now, if you have kids and they are anything like my little chick, Indie, it's hard to drag them away from their toys, tablets and books. But when the aromas start to waft around the house, they will soon come running.

One of my favourite dishes growing up was a classic spaghetti Bolognese complete with that awful dried Parmesan you had to shake out of a cardboard tube. Adults and kids alike will love my Slow-Cooked Beef Ragù version, but I ask you one thing: please use fresh Parmesan cheese to grate over the top!

THREE CHEESE MAC WITH CHORIZO CRUMB

Mac 'n' cheese has had a massive renaissance in recent years. In fact, you would probably be hard pressed to find a trendy restaurant without it on the menu. My version is a real cheat's treat. Out goes the time-consuming white sauce and in comes time-saving store cupboard ingredients. I promise that the whole family will love this one – the team on the photo shoot demolished it in minutes.

SERVES 4

400 g (14 oz) dried macaroni pasta

1 x 410 g (14½ oz) can of evaporated milk

600 ml (20 fl oz) milk (slow cooker method only)

100 g (3½ oz) Cheddar cheese, grated

100 g (3½ oz) Monterey Jack cheese, grated

50 g (1¾ oz) Parmesan cheese, grated

4 tablespoons tomato ketchup

1 teaspoon Dijon mustard

½ teaspoon garlic powder

Couple of drops of hot sauce (optional)

Salt and pepper

Crisp side salad, to serve

Chorizo crumb:

3 tablespoons olive oil or 40 g (1½ oz) butter

100 g (3½ oz) chorizo sausage, cut into very small dice

1 small ciabatta roll, grated or blitzed to large crumbs

CONVENTIONAL METHOD

1 Preheat the oven to 190°C (375°F), Gas Mark 5.
2 Cook the macaroni according to the packet instructions. Drain and set aside.
3 While the pasta is cooking, make the chorizo crumb. Heat the oil or butter in a pan, then add the chorizo and cook for a couple of minutes. Throw in the breadcrumbs and cook over a medium heat for 1 minute. Remove from the heat and set aside.
4 Pour the evaporated milk into a separate pan, then add two-thirds of the grated cheese along with the ketchup, mustard and garlic powder and stir until melted. Season and add hot sauce to taste (if using). Add the pasta and stir to make sure it's well combined. Transfer to an ovenproof baking dish, then sprinkle with the remaining cheese and the chorizo crumb.
5 Bake in the oven for 20 minutes, until golden. Leave to stand for a few minutes before serving with a crisp side salad.

SLOW COOKER METHOD

1 Pop your pasta into your slow cooker, then add the evaporated milk, milk and two-thirds of the grated cheese along with the ketchup, mustard and garlic powder. Season and add hot sauce to taste (if using) and stir well. Press down to make sure the pasta is submerged.
2 Cook on the low setting for 2 hours. Remove the lid, stir and add a little more milk if it needs it, then scatter over the remaining cheese. Cook for a further 30 minutes.
3 To make the chorizo crumb, heat the oil or butter in a pan, then add the chorizo and cook for a couple of minutes. Throw in the breadcrumbs and cook over a medium heat for 3–4 minutes, until golden.
4 Scatter the chorizo crumb over the mac 'n' cheese. Serve with a crisp side salad.

CAPRESE CHICKEN MELT

Something magical happens when you roast tomatoes – the already sweet tomatoes start to dry out and the flavour intensifies tenfold. This recipe is based on one of my favourite dishes, the Caprese salad of tomato, mozzarella and basil. I'm not quite sure how these three humble ingredients can be such an incredible taste sensation when eaten together, but I'm not going to complain. You can put all the ingredients uncooked into your slow cooker for ease, but I like to start the process in a pan because I find that the tomatoes release too much liquid into the pot.

SERVES 4

1–2 tablespoons olive oil
4 chicken breasts, skin on
1 red onion, thinly sliced
200 g (7 oz) baby plum tomatoes, halved
1 x 150 g (5½ oz) ball of mozzarella, sliced
1 small ciabatta roll, torn into chunks
Small bunch of basil, shredded
Salt and pepper

Dressing:
4 teaspoons olive oil
4 teaspoons balsamic vinegar
1 tablespoon runny honey
2 garlic cloves, crushed

To serve:
Sauté potatoes
Crisp side salad

CONVENTIONAL METHOD

1 Preheat the oven to 180°C (350°F), Gas Mark 4.
2 Heat the oil in a large shallow ovenproof pan set over a medium to high heat. Add the chicken breasts, skin side down, and cook for 3–4 minutes, until golden. Remove from the pan, then pop in the onion and tomatoes, reduce the heat and cook for a few minutes.
3 Add the chicken breasts back in, season with salt and pepper and transfer to the oven. Cook, uncovered, for 20 minutes.
4 While the chicken is in the oven, whisk together the oil, vinegar, honey and garlic for the dressing. Remove the pan from the oven, then pour over the dressing. Place the slices of mozzarella on the chicken breasts, season with a little more pepper and scatter in the torn ciabatta. Return to the oven and cook for a further 10 minutes, until the chicken has cooked through.
5 Before serving, scatter over the fresh basil. Serve with some sauté potatoes and a crisp salad on the side.

SLOW COOKER METHOD

1 Follow step 2 as above.
2 Scatter the cooked onion and tomatoes in your slow cooker, then season with salt and pepper. Place the golden chicken breasts on top, pop on the lid and cook on the low setting for 4½ hours.
3 While the chicken is in the slow cooker, whisk together the oil, vinegar, honey and garlic for the dressing.
4 Once the cooking time has elapsed, pour the dressing over the chicken, onion and tomatoes, then lay the mozzarella on the chicken breasts, pop the lid back on and cook on the high setting for a further 30 minutes.
5 Preheat the oven to 180°C (350°F), Gas Mark 4. Place the ciabatta chunks on a baking tray and cook in the oven for 10 minutes. Before serving the chicken, scatter over the croutons and fresh basil. Serve with some sauté potatoes and a crisp salad on the side.

LOADED BAKED HASSELBACK SWEET POTATOES

Like many people I got into eating sweet potatoes in a big way a few years ago. I like them roasted, wedged, mashed, chipped or, my favourite, baked! Cooked this way, they become almost sticky in texture. Load them whichever way you like – even a simple knob of butter is delicious, but I love to go way over the top with cheese, smoky chorizo and soured cream to cut through the richness. You have to try these.

SERVES 4

4 medium sweet potatoes, unpeeled
2 tablespoons olive oil
2 tablespoons garlic butter, melted
150 g (5½ oz) Cheddar cheese, thinly sliced
100 g (3½ oz) chorizo sausage, cubed
150 ml (¼ pint) soured cream
4 spring onions, thinly sliced
1 jalapeño, deseeded and thinly sliced (optional)
Salt and pepper

CONVENTIONAL METHOD

1 Preheat the oven to 180°C (350°F), Gas Mark 4. Line a baking sheet with foil.
2 Slice the sweet potatoes at 2 cm (¾ inch) intervals, cutting two-thirds of the way down. Aim for 6–7 cuts per potato. Rub the potatoes with the oil, making sure you get a good coating, then season with a pinch of salt and pepper.
3 Place on the foil-lined baking sheet and roast in the oven for 45 minutes. Remove from the oven, then run a fork across the top of the potatoes to fan them out. Brush over the garlic butter, then place some thin slices of Cheddar in between alternate cuts in the potato. Return to the oven for 10 minutes, until the cheese has melted.
4 Meanwhile, fry the chorizo in a dry pan over a medium heat until golden. This will take 3–4 minutes.
5 Pop the potatoes onto serving plates, then drizzle over the soured cream and sprinkle over the crispy chorizo, spring onions and jalapeño. I also like to drizzle over any chorizo oil left in the pan from frying.

SLOW COOKER METHOD

1 Follow step 2 as above.
2 Line your slow cooker with a large sheet of nonstick baking paper – just scrunch it in there, don't be too precise. Add the potatoes, put on the lid and cook on the high setting for 4 hours.
3 Remove the potatoes from the slow cooker and run a fork across the top of them to fan them out. Brush over the garlic butter, then place some thin slices of Cheddar in between alternate cuts in the potato. Return to the slow cooker and leave the lid slightly ajar. Cook for a further 30 minutes, until the cheese has melted.
4 Follow steps 4–5 as above.

TIP

Make sure you line your baking sheet with foil if using the conventional method, otherwise it will be very difficult to clean.

STICKY CHERRY COLA BABY BACK RIBS

The thing we all look for when tucking in to a rack of sticky glazed pork ribs is for the meat to literally fall from the bone. The only way to achieve this is to cook them very slowly. The traditional American way is to smoke them gently in a pit or barbecue, but with a little love you can replicate that flavour with amazing results in your oven or slow cooker. It starts with a dry rub and finishes with a sticky cola glaze. It also works really well with other soda flavours, like dandelion and burdock or ginger beer. Just don't use a sugar-free cola or soda, otherwise it won't reduce down to a syrup.

SERVES 4

2 racks of baby back ribs, approx.
　1 kg (2 lb 4 oz)
Spring onions, sliced, to serve

Dry rub:
1 tablespoon smoked paprika
1 tablespoon garlic powder
1 tablespoon ground black pepper
1 teaspoon salt

Cherry cola barbecue sauce:
1 small onion, finely diced
2 garlic cloves, crushed
1 x 330 ml (11½ fl oz) can of cherry
　cola
100 ml (3½ fl oz) barbecue sauce
1 heaped tablespoon tomato purée
1 tablespoon grated fresh root
　ginger

CONVENTIONAL METHOD

1 Prepare the racks by removing the membrane from the back of the ribs. Mix all the dry rub ingredients together in a bowl. Place the ribs on a baking tray and sprinkle over the dry rub, then massage it in until the ribs are covered. Wrap the ribs in clingfilm and leave to marinate for as long as you can – overnight would be great.
2 Preheat the oven to 150°C (300°F), Gas Mark 2.
3 Remove the ribs from the clingfilm and wrap tightly in a double layer of foil. Pop the wrapped ribs on a clean baking tray and put into the oven to cook for 3 hours.
4 When the ribs come out of the oven, preheat the grill.
5 Put all the cola barbecue sauce ingredients in a pan and reduce down until thick and syrupy.
6 Remove the ribs from the foil and place them under the hot grill for a few minutes, basting frequently with the barbecue sauce. Serve with a scattering of spring onions.

SLOW COOKER METHOD

1 Follow step 1 as above.
2 Mix together all the cola barbecue sauce ingredients in a small bowl.
3 Place the ribs vertically in your slow cooker, thicker side down and with the meatier side facing the interior of the pot. Pour the barbecue sauce over the ribs, then cover with the lid and cook on the low setting for 8 hours.
4 Preheat the grill.
5 Gently remove the ribs from the slow cooker, then pour the liquid into a pan and reduce until thickened. At this point you can place the ribs under the hot grill for a few minutes, basting frequently with the barbecue sauce. Serve with a scattering of spring onions.

SLOW-COOKED BEEF RAGÙ

I've tried out so many Bolognese and ragù recipes over the years, but this one truly is the best. Okay, there may be a few ingredients in here, like the milk, that might sound strange, but trust me, it works. The milk adds a real richness to this ultimate version of a family classic. I love to serve this with crispy fried gnocchi, a generous grating of Parmesan cheese and some freshly torn basil.

SERVES 4

1–2 tablespoons olive oil

600 g (1 lb 5 oz) skirt steak, cut into 2.5 cm (1 inch) cubes

2 tablespoons plain flour seasoned with salt and pepper

100 g (3½ oz) smoked pancetta or smoked streaky bacon, cubed

2 onions, finely diced

1 large carrot, finely diced

3 celery sticks, finely diced

5 garlic cloves, crushed

1 tablespoon finely chopped fresh rosemary

100 ml (3½ fl oz) milk

2 heaped tablespoons tomato purée

200 ml (⅓ pint) white wine

600 ml (20 fl oz) beef stock if using the conventional method or 400 ml (14 fl oz) if using the slow cooker method

Pinch of caster sugar

Salt and pepper

To serve:

1 tablespoon olive oil

2 x 400 g (14 oz) shop-bought packs of potato gnocchi

Parmesan cheese, grated

Basil leaves, torn

CONVENTIONAL METHOD

1 Preheat the oven to 160°C (325°F), Gas Mark 3.

2 Heat the oil in a large heavy-based casserole over a high heat. Dust the beef in the seasoned flour, then place in the casserole and cook for 4–5 minutes, until golden. Remove from the pot and set aside.

3 Reduce the heat to low to medium. Add the pancetta, onions, carrot, celery, garlic and rosemary and cook for 6–7 minutes, until softened. Pour in the milk and reduce until it has evaporated. Stir through the tomato purée for a couple of minutes, then pour in the white wine and reduce by half.

4 Add the beef back in along with 600 ml (20 fl oz) of stock and stir to combine. Bring up to a gentle simmer, then cover with a tight-fitting lid and cook in the oven for 4 hours, checking along the way and adding a splash of water if needed. Before serving, season with salt, pepper and sugar to taste. Use forks to shred some of the larger chunks of meat.

5 To cook the gnocchi, add a splash of oil to a large frying pan over a medium heat. Add the gnocchi and cook for 3–4 minutes on each side, until golden and crispy.

6 Serve the ragù with the crispy gnocchi, with some freshly grated Parmesan and torn basil leaves scattered over.

SLOW COOKER METHOD

1 Follow steps 2–3 as above.

2 Spoon the vegetables into your slow cooker, then add the beef. Pour in the 400 ml (14 fl oz) of stock and stir well. Cover with your lid and cook on the low setting for 8 hours. Before serving, season with salt, pepper and sugar to taste.

3 Follow steps 5–6 as above.

HUNGARIAN GOULASH

I'm going to let you in on a secret: I used to adore school dinners. Cheese Scotch eggs, Spam fritters, Australian crunch with mint custard and chocolate semolina were among my favourites. The lunch I loved best, though, was the school's take on Hungarian goulash. The tender beef was just the thing to warm me up on those freezing cold dinner breaks. In school it was all about rice, but I think a buttery mash spiked with some horseradish sauce can't be beaten with my deep, smoky goulash.

SERVES 4

1–2 tablespoons olive oil

800 g (1 lb 12 oz) beef shin, cut into
   2.5 cm (1 inch) cubes

1 tablespoon plain flour seasoned with
   salt and pepper

1 onion, sliced

1 red pepper, sliced

1 garlic clove, crushed

1 heaped tablespoon tomato purée

1 heaped teaspoon regular paprika

1 teaspoon smoked paprika

1 bay leaf

1 x 400 g (14 oz) can of chopped
   tomatoes

500 ml (18 fl oz) beef stock if using
   the conventional method or 200 ml
   (⅓ pint) if using the slow cooker
   method

1 teaspoon caster sugar (or to taste)

Salt and pepper

CONVENTIONAL METHOD

1 Preheat the oven to 140°C (275°F), Gas Mark 1.

2 Heat the oil in a large heavy-based casserole over a high heat. Dust the meat in the seasoned flour, then add to the casserole and fry for 5–6 minutes, until golden. You may need to do this in batches so you don't overcrowd the pan. Remove and set aside.

3 Reduce the heat to low to medium, then add the onion and red pepper and cook for 5 minutes, adding a little more oil if necessary. Pop in the garlic and cook for a minute, then add the tomato purée, spices and bay leaf. (Or you could use the Time Saver Garlic Base and skip frying the onion and garlic here.) Stir for a couple of minutes, then pour in the chopped tomatoes and 500 ml (18 fl oz) of stock. Add the beef back to the pot along with some salt and pepper and stir well.

4 Put on a tight-fitting lid and cook in the oven for 4 hours. Check the seasoning, then add the sugar to taste.

5 Serve with soured cream and parsley and some buttery mashed potatoes with a little horseradish sauce stirred in.

TIME SAVER TIP
Use 1 portion of the Time Saver
Garlic Base on page 14 instead
of the onion and garlic.

To serve:

Soured cream

Fresh parsley

Mashed potatoes spiked with
  horseradish sauce

SLOW COOKER METHOD

1 Follow step 2 for the conventional method opposite.

2 Place the onion, red pepper and garlic in your slow cooker (or use the Time
Saver Garlic Base), then add the rest of the ingredients except the sugar,
making sure you use only 200 ml (⅓ pint) of stock, and stir well. Stir through
the beef, then season with salt and pepper. Pop on the lid and cook on the low
setting for 6 hours.

3 Check the seasoning, then add the sugar to taste.

4 Follow step 5 for the conventional method opposite.

SOMERSET CIDER BRAISED CHICKEN

I'm a Bristolian born and bred, and for any of you who have caught me cooking on TV, my strong country bumpkin accent will testify to that. Here in the West Country there's something we do better than anyone else in the entire world – we make incredible cider! I use cider in my cooking all the time, from the Christmas turkey gravy to this delicious, comforting braised chicken recipe. You will love this so much that a trip to Somerset will be on the cards.

SERVES 4

1–2 tablespoons olive oil

600 g (1 lb 5 oz) skinless chicken thighs, bone in

2 tablespoons plain flour seasoned with salt and pepper

12 shallots, peeled

1 small leek, shredded

2 garlic cloves, crushed

300 ml (½ pint) cider if using the conventional method or 200 ml (⅓ pint) if using the slow cooker method

300 ml (½ pint) chicken stock if using the conventional method or 200 ml (⅓ pint) if using the slow cooker method

1 tablespoon wholegrain mustard

700 g (1 lb 9 oz) new potatoes, halved

200 g (7 oz) frozen peas

2 heaped tablespoons crème fraîche

Salt and pepper

To serve:
Mashed potatoes
Shredded Savoy cabbage

CONVENTIONAL METHOD

1 Preheat the oven to 170°C (340°F), Gas Mark 3.
2 Heat the oil in a large heavy-based casserole over a medium to high heat. Dust the chicken thighs in the seasoned flour, then add to the casserole and cook for 4–5 minutes, until golden. Add the shallots, leek and garlic, then pour in the 300 ml (½ pint) of cider and 300 ml (½ pint) of stock. Stir through the mustard, then add the potatoes. Add a pinch of salt and pepper and bring up to a simmer. Put on a tight-fitting lid and cook in the oven for 2 hours.
3 Remove from the oven and scatter in the peas. Pop the lid back on and leave to sit for 5 minutes, then stir through the crème fraîche.
4 Serve with mash and some peppery shredded Savoy cabbage.

SLOW COOKER METHOD

1 Heat the oil in a large pan over a medium to high heat. Dust the chicken thighs in the seasoned flour, then fry in the pan until golden. Add the shallots, leek and garlic and cook for a further 5 minutes.
2 Transfer to your slow cooker, then pour in the 200 ml (⅓ pint) of cider and 200 ml (⅓ pint) of stock. Stir through the mustard and add the potatoes. Add a pinch of salt and pepper, then put on the lid and cook on the low setting for 6 hours.
3 Scatter in the peas and cook for a further 10 minutes before correcting the seasoning and stirring through the crème fraîche.
4 Follow step 4 as above.

FISH STEW BOUILLABAISSE

This beautiful, vibrant fish stew takes its influence from the classic bouillabaisse. Hints of aniseed coming from the fennel and Pernod work perfectly with fish. You can use pretty much whatever firm fish or shellfish you like in this recipe, but make sure it's all cut to the same size so it cooks at the same rate. The classic accompaniments are toasted slices of baguette spread with rouille – a punchy, garlicky sauce that's thickened with breadcrumbs and has a hit of saffron and cayenne too.

SERVES 4

1–2 tablespoons olive oil

1 onion, finely diced

1 fennel bulb, sliced (save the green fronds for garnish)

2 garlic cloves, crushed

1 red chilli, deseeded and diced

2 tablespoons Pernod (optional)

1 heaped tablespoon tomato purée

1 x 400 g (14 oz) can of chopped tomatoes

300 g (10½ oz) Maris Piper potatoes, cubed

700 ml (1¼ pints) fish or vegetable stock if using the conventional method or 300 ml (½ pint) if using the slow cooker method

1 teaspoon paprika

1 teaspoon caster sugar (or to taste)

400 g (14 oz) skinless firm fish fillets, such as salmon, haddock, red mullet or monkfish

165 g (5¾ oz) raw prawns

Salt and pepper

To serve:

Toasted baguette slices

Rouille

CONVENTIONAL METHOD

1   Heat the oil in a large heavy-based casserole over a low to medium heat. Add the onion, fennel, garlic and chilli and fry for around 10 minutes, until softened. Add the Pernod (if using) and reduce until it has nearly evaporated. Stir in the tomato purée and cook for a further minute.

2   Add the tomatoes, potatoes, 700 ml (1¼ pints) of stock and the paprika, then cook over a very low heat for 1 hour. Season with salt, pepper and the sugar.

3   Add the fish and prawns, then put on a lid and cook for around 10 minutes, until the fish is cooked through.

4   Spoon into serving bowls and garnish with the reserved fennel fronds. Serve with toasted baguette slices spread with rouille.

SLOW COOKER METHOD

1   Follow step 1 as above, then transfer to your slow cooker along with the tomatoes, potatoes, 300 ml (½ pint) of stock and the paprika. Season with salt and pepper, then cover and cook on the low setting for 6 hours.

2   Add the sugar to taste, then turn the heat setting to high. Add the fish and prawns and cook for a further 10 minutes.

3   Follow step 4 as above.

CREOLE CHICKEN AND SHRIMP GUMBO

This New Orleans-inspired gumbo relies on a nutty roux (a mixture of butter and flour) as a thickener. This step should be done in a heavy-based pan because it will need to cook gently and not burn while achieving a beautiful dark, nutty colour. You can then cook this dish in the oven or pop all the ingredients into your slow cooker to tick away gently until the punchy Creole flavours meld together.

SERVES 4

30 g (1 oz) unsalted butter
30 g (1 oz) plain flour
100 g (3½ oz) chorizo sausage, diced
1 onion, finely diced
1 green pepper, finely diced
2 celery sticks, finely diced
4 garlic cloves, crushed
2 bay leaves
1 teaspoon smoked paprika
1 teaspoon ground cumin
100 ml (3½ fl oz) white wine
1 x 500 ml (18 fl oz) carton of tomato
    passata
400 ml (14 fl oz) chicken stock if
    using the conventional method
    or 200 ml (⅓ pint) if using the slow
    cooker method
4 boneless, skinless chicken thighs
200 g (7 oz) raw prawns
Pinch of caster sugar (optional)
Salt and pepper

To garnish:
Soured cream (optional)
3 tablespoons chopped flat leaf
    parsley
5 spring onions, sliced

To serve:
Boiled rice
Crusty bread

CONVENTIONAL METHOD

1   Preheat the oven to 160°C (325°F), Gas Mark 3.
2   Combine the butter and flour in a large heavy-based casserole and cook over a low to medium heat for 10–15 minutes, stirring frequently. The roux needs to be a nutty brown colour.
3   Place the diced chorizo, onion, green pepper, celery and garlic in the casserole. Cook for 6–7 minutes, until softened. Add the bay leaves, paprika and cumin and stir for a minute before pouring in the white wine and reducing by half.
4   Add the passata and 400 ml (14 fl oz) of stock and bring to a simmer. Gently add the chicken thighs, then cover the casserole with a tight-fitting lid and cook in the oven for 3 hours.
5   Remove the lid and stir in the prawns, then cover again and leave to stand for 5 minutes. Season to taste with salt, pepper and a pinch of sugar if needed. Garnish with a dollop of soured cream and the parsley and spring onions. Serve with boiled rice and crusty bread.

SLOW COOKER METHOD

1   Follow step 2 as above, then add the roux to the slow cooker. Follow step 3 as well, if you have time. If not, pop all the ingredients except the prawns and sugar in with the roux and stir well, making sure you use only 200 ml (⅓ pint) of stock. Put the lid on and cook on the low setting for 6 hours.
2   Stir in the prawns, then continue cooking with the lid slightly ajar for a further 30 minutes. Season with salt, pepper and a pinch of sugar if needed. Garnish with a dollop of soured cream and the parsley and spring onions. Serve with boiled rice and crusty bread.

STICKY HOISIN DUCK DOGS

One of the dishes I loved as a kid was crispy duck pancakes loaded with spring onions and cucumber batons and liberally drizzled with sweet and sticky hoisin sauce. It's one of those combinations of ingredients that's just so delicious. My addition of the lightly pickled cucumber really cuts through the rich, sweet duck, and once you see how well this works, you'll never go back. The chilli is an optional extra that I love, but of course feel free to leave it out if you don't enjoy that kick of heat.

SERVES 4

4 duck legs
1 heaped teaspoon Chinese
   five-spice powder
1 teaspoon salt
150 ml (¼ pint) chicken stock
Juice of 1 orange
3 tablespoons hoisin sauce, plus
   extra to serve

Pickled cucumber:
80 ml (2¾ fl oz) rice wine vinegar
   or apple cider vinegar
50 g (1¾ oz) caster sugar
¼ cucumber, deseeded and diced
½ red chilli, deseeded and diced

To serve:
8 brioche hot dog rolls
4 spring onions, shredded

CONVENTIONAL METHOD

1 Prick the skin of the duck legs all over with a fork, then rub well with the five-spice and salt. Place in the refrigerator for at least 2 hours or overnight if possible.
2 Preheat the oven to 200°C (400°F), Gas Mark 6.
3 To make the cucumber pickle, pour the vinegar into a small pan along with the sugar and bring to the boil, stirring until the sugar has dissolved. Leave to cool, then add the diced cucumber and chilli. Set aside.
4 Pat the duck legs dry with kitchen paper, then place in a dry frying pan and cook over a medium heat for 10–12 minutes, until golden. At this stage you are trying to render some of the fat from the duck. Remove the duck from the pan and transfer to a roasting tin. Keep the fat from your frying pan for delicious roast potatoes.
5 Pour the stock and orange juice into the tin, then pop in the oven to cook for 20 minutes. Reduce the heat to 150°C (300°F), Gas Mark 2, cover the tin with foil and cook for 2 hours.
6 Remove from the oven and allow to cool slightly before shredding the duck into a bowl. Mix through the hoisin sauce and a little of the cooking juices from the tin.
7 Portion the shredded duck into the hot dog rolls, then drizzle over more hoisin sauce and scatter over the spring onions and pickled cucumber.

SLOW COOKER METHOD

1 Follow steps 1, 3 and 4 as above.
2 Pour the stock and orange juice into your slow cooker, then add the duck. Put the lid on and cook on the low setting for 8 hours.
3 Remove the duck from the slow cooker and allow to cool slightly before shredding into a bowl. Mix through the hoisin sauce and a little of the cooking juices from the pot.
4 Follow step 7 as above.

ITALIAN POLENTA BAKE

This is one of those recipes that may offend foodie purists because it's a combination of two ideas and two cultures. It's kind of like an Italian-inspired cottage pie, with a beautiful smoky tomato-based mince topped with a crispy Parmesan polenta instead of the traditional mash. Before you shoot me down, please give this one a go with an open mind – I know you will love it.

SERVES 4

500 g (1 lb 2 oz) minced beef
100 g (3½ oz) smoked pancetta or smoked streaky bacon, cubed
2 onions, finely diced
1 large carrot, finely diced
4 garlic cloves, crushed
1 tablespoon finely chopped fresh rosemary
200 ml (⅓ pint) red wine
1 x 500 g (1 lb 2 oz) carton of tomato passata
200 ml (⅓ pint) beef stock (conventional method only)
1 heaped tablespoon tomato purée
1 tablespoon dried oregano
Pinch of caster sugar
Salt and pepper

Topping:
600 ml (20 fl oz) vegetable stock
100 g (3½ oz) polenta
100 g (3½ oz) Parmesan cheese, grated
50 g (1¾ oz) butter

To serve:
Grated Parmesan
Crisp side salad
Garlic bread

CONVENTIONAL METHOD

1 Place the minced beef in a hot, dry, large heavy-based casserole and cook for 5–6 minutes over a high heat, until golden. Remove from the pan and set aside. Add the pancetta, onions, carrot, garlic and rosemary and cook for 6–7 minutes before returning the mince to the casserole. Pour in the red wine and reduce by half. Add the passata, beef stock, tomato purée and oregano and stir to combine. Bring up to a simmer, then cover with a lid and cook over a low heat for 1 hour. Season with salt, pepper and a good pinch of sugar.

2 To make the topping, bring the vegetable stock to the boil in a separate large pan, then gradually pour in the polenta, whisking as you go. Cook over a medium heat for 5–6 minutes, whisking constantly, until thickened. Remove from the heat and stir through the Parmesan and butter. Taste and season with salt and pepper.

3 Preheat the oven to 180°C (350°F), Gas Mark 4.

4 Spoon the polenta over the mince and level it out. Cook in the oven for 20 minutes.

5 Leave to stand for 5 minutes, then serve with a grating of fresh Parmesan on top and a crisp salad and garlic bread on the side.

SLOW COOKER METHOD

1 Place the minced beef into a preheated pan and cook for 5–6 minutes over a high heat, until golden. Add the pancetta, onions, carrot, garlic and rosemary and cook for 5 minutes, then pour in the wine and reduce by half. Decant into your slow cooker along with the passata, tomato purée and oregano. Cover and cook on the low setting for 6 hours.

2 Follow step 2 as for the conventional method opposite to make the polenta, then spoon this on top of the beef in your slow cooker and level it out. Turn the temperature up to high and cook for an additional 30 minutes with the lid slightly ajar.

3 Follow step 5 as for the conventional method opposite.

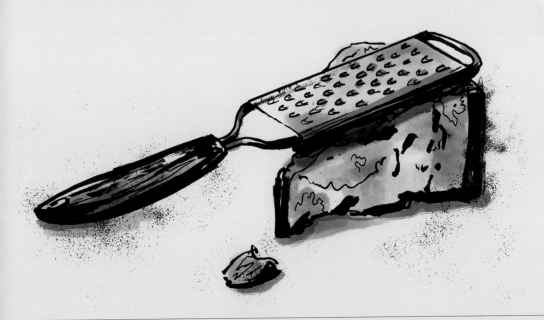

CHAR SUI SHREDDED BEEF

I love the pungent aromas that waft through the house while this beef is cooking. The other thing I love about this recipe is that it really needs no prep – it's definitely the kind of dish where you can throw it all in and leave it to do its thing. I use skirt steak in this one (sometimes called pasty steak), which is readily available in your local butcher or supermarket. Best of all, it's cheap and when cooked slowly it melts in your mouth.

SERVES 4

1–2 tablespoons olive oil
600 g (1 lb 5 oz) skirt steak
1 onion, sliced
½ teaspoon cornflour
4 teaspoons water

Braising liquor:
4 garlic cloves, crushed
1 thumb-sized piece of fresh root
   ginger, grated
200 ml (⅓ pint) beef stock if using
   the conventional method or
   100 ml (3½ fl oz) if using the
   slow cooker method
50 ml (2 fl oz) hoisin sauce
4 tablespoons Chinese rice wine
   or dry sherry
2 tablespoons soy sauce
2 tablespoons sweet chilli sauce
1 tablespoon tomato purée
1 star anise
½ teaspoon Chinese five-spice
   powder

To serve:
Fried rice
4 spring onions, sliced
1 tablespoon sesame seeds

CONVENTIONAL METHOD

1 Preheat the oven to 160°C (325°F), Gas Mark 3.
2 Combine all the braising liquor ingredients in a bowl, making sure you use 200 ml (⅓ pint) of stock, and whisk until fully combined.
3 Heat the oil in a large heavy-based casserole over a medium to high heat. Add the skirt steak and sear for 3–4 minutes, then remove and set aside. Place the sliced onion in the bottom of the casserole, then place the seared steak on top. Pour over the braising liquor, cover with a tight-fitting lid and cook in the oven for 3 hours.
4 Remove from the oven and use forks to shred the meat. Combine the cornflour with the water, then add this to the beef and stir it through to thicken the sauce.
5 Serve the shredded beef with fried rice and sprinkle over the spring onions and toasted sesame seeds.

SLOW COOKER METHOD

1 Follow step 2 as above, making sure you use only 100 ml (3½ fl oz) of stock, then pour this into your slow cooker. Scatter in the onion, then place the beef on top. Pop on the lid and cook on the low setting for 7 hours.
2 Use forks to shred the meat. Combine the cornflour with the water, then add this to the beef and stir it through to thicken the sauce.
3 Follow step 5 as above.

CARIBBEAN LAMB CURRY

I adore curry and I've always been a bit of a sucker for a good chilli hit, but the complexity of flavours in this makes it one of my absolute favourites because the sweet potatoes balance out the spicy ingredients. Pair this with some rice and beans and an ice-cold lager (adults only) to get a true taste of Caribbean sunshine.

SERVES 4

1–2 tablespoons olive oil

500 g (1 lb 2 oz) lamb shoulder, cut into 2.5 cm (1 inch) cubes

1 tablespoon plain flour seasoned with salt and pepper

1 large onion, finely diced

4 garlic cloves, crushed

1 tablespoon grated fresh root ginger

1 x 400 ml (14 fl oz) can of coconut milk

400 ml (14 fl oz) lamb stock if using the conventional method or 200 ml (⅓ pint) if using the slow cooker method

4 thyme sprigs, leaves picked

2 tablespoons red wine vinegar

2 tablespoons Worcestershire sauce

1 heaped tablespoon jerk paste

1 tablespoon light brown sugar

1 teaspoon ground allspice

½ teaspoon ground cinnamon

2 sweet potatoes, diced

1 green pepper, cut into large dice

1 red pepper, cut into large dice

Salt and pepper

Fresh coriander, finely chopped, to garnish

Rice and beans, to serve

CONVENTIONAL METHOD

1   Heat the oil in a large heavy-based casserole over a medium to high heat. Dust the lamb in the flour, then fry in batches for 5–6 minutes, until browned. Set aside.
2   In the same casserole, cook the onion, garlic and ginger (or Time Saver Curry Base) in a little more oil for 5 minutes. Add the coconut milk, 400 ml (14 fl oz) of stock, thyme, vinegar, Worcestershire sauce, jerk paste, brown sugar and spices. Bring up to a simmer, then return the lamb to the pot and add the sweet potatoes.
3   Put a lid on and cook over a very low heat for 3 hours. Remove the lid and add the green and red peppers, then cook for a further 20 minutes with the lid off to allow the sauce to thicken.
4   Season with salt and pepper, then garnish with finely chopped fresh coriander and serve with rice and beans on the side.

SLOW COOKER METHOD

1   Follow step 1 as above.
2   Put all the ingredients except the green and red peppers and fresh coriander in your slow cooker, making sure you use only 200 ml (⅓ pint) of stock. Put on the lid and cook on the low setting for 7 hours.
3   Add the peppers, then cook for 1 hour more.
4   Follow step 4 as above.

TIME SAVER TIP
You could use 1 portion of the Time Saver Curry Base on page 14 instead of the onion, garlic and ginger.

SLOW COOKER VEGETABLE LASAGNE

There are a few stages to this recipe, but it's not complicated. However, the stages are important. It's key that you cook the mushrooms until golden and griddle the courgettes, otherwise the lasagne will be watery and not the flavour-packed delight it could be with a little time and effort. That's really what this book is about: taking your time to achieve spectacular results. I serve this with a simple dressed salad and, if I'm pushing the boat out, a lovely garlic loaf.

SERVES 4

1–2 tablespoons olive oil

200 g (7 oz) mushrooms, trimmed and sliced

2 red peppers, finely diced

1 onion, finely diced

4 garlic cloves, crushed

1 tablespoon dried oregano

1 x 500 ml (18 fl oz) carton of tomato passata

300 ml (½ pint) vegetable stock if using the conventional method or 150 ml (¼ pint) if using the slow cooker method

1 tablespoon tomato purée

3 courgettes, thinly sliced lengthways

200 g (7 oz) Parmesan cheese, grated

1 tomato, thinly sliced

Salt and pepper

White sauce:
50 g (1¾ oz) unsalted butter
50 g (1¾ oz) plain flour
600 ml (20 fl oz) milk

To serve:
Simple dressed salad
Garlic bread

CONVENTIONAL METHOD

1 Preheat the oven to 190°C (375°F), Gas Mark 5.

2 Heat the oil in a frying pan over a high heat. Add the mushrooms and fry for 6–7 minutes, until golden, then set aside. Cook the red peppers, onion and garlic in the same pan for 5 minutes. Sprinkle in the oregano and give it a good stir before adding the passata, 300 ml (½ pint) of stock, the tomato purée and returning the mushrooms to the pan. Bring up to a simmer and cook, uncovered, for 15 minutes. Season with salt and pepper.

3 Meanwhile, griddle the courgette slices on a ridged pan for 1–2 minutes on each side, until charred. Set aside.

4 To make the white sauce, melt the butter over a medium heat, then whisk in the flour and cook for 2–3 minutes. Gradually pour in the milk and continue whisking until thickened and smooth. Season well with salt and pepper.

5 Spoon a layer of the mushroom mixture into a 25 cm x 18 cm (10 inch x 7 inch) baking dish. Top with a layer of the griddled courgettes, then some of the white sauce, then sprinkle over some of the grated Parmesan. Repeat until all the ingredients have been used up, but make sure you finish with a layer of white sauce and keep back some of the cheese. Scatter on the remaining Parmesan, then add a layer of tomato slices.

6 Cook in the oven for 40 minutes. Leave to stand for a good 10 minutes before serving with a simple dressed salad and garlic bread.

SLOW COOKER METHOD

1 Follow steps 2–4 as for the conventional method opposite, making sure you use only 150 ml (¼ pint) of stock.

2 Spoon a layer of the mushroom mixture into your slow cooker. Top with a layer of the griddled courgettes, then some of the white sauce, then sprinkle over some of the grated Parmesan. Repeat until all the ingredients have been used up, but make sure you finish with a layer of white sauce and keep back some of the cheese. Scatter on the remaining Parmesan, then add a layer of tomato slices. Pop the lid on and cook on the high setting for 4 hours.

3 Serve with a simple dressed salad and garlic bread.

Feel Good Food

This is the sort of food that not only makes you feel good eating it, but is also immensely satisfying to prepare. I love that feeling that comes from prepping the ingredients, much of which can be done in advance, from dicing onions and making curry pastes to shredding fresh herbs. And at the end of that process you deliver a delicious, healthy meal to the table that everyone will love.

The recipes in this chapter are packed full of fresh ingredients, including recipes for the most skipped meal: breakfast. This is the meal that sets you up for the day and gives you the energy to face whatever life throws at you head on. Okay, I guess some of you prefer an extra five minutes in bed, but what could be easier than coming down the stairs in the morning to a steaming bowl of creamy porridge or my lazy Sunday morning Breakfast Shakshuka?

Chillies also make me feel good. When we eat chillies, our brains release endorphins, the feel-good happy hormones, so immediately food can be that pick-me-up that puts a shine on the day. I use this excuse for constantly eating Roy's Famous Off-the-Menu Hot Wings!

OVERNIGHT SLOW COOKER OATS

I've included two of my favourite overnight porridge recipes here. The porridge can be made three ways: the conventional way in a pan, stirring as you go; in the slow cooker overnight; or placed in the refrigerator overnight for a cool uncooked breakfast, which is great in the summer. The smell of the spiced apple or comforting cocoa as you come downstairs in the morning is worth jumping out of bed for. Plus the filling porridge will set you up with enough slow-releasing energy to tackle the day ahead.

SERVES 1

Spiced apple porridge:
1 apple, peeled and diced small
40 g (1½ oz) rolled oats
30 g (1 oz) dried cranberries
250–350ml (9–12fl oz) milk if using the conventional or uncooked method, or 500 ml (18 fl oz) if using the slow cooker method
1 tablespoon honey (or to taste)
¼ teaspoon ground cinnamon

Chocolate pr-oat-in porridge:
40 g (1½ oz) rolled oats
250–350ml (9–12fl oz) milk or almond milk if using the conventional or uncooked method, or 500 ml (18 fl oz) if using the slow cooker method
1 scoop of vanilla or chocolate protein powder
1 heaped teaspoon cocoa powder

CONVENTIONAL METHOD

1 Place the porridge oats into a saucepan along with the milk then bring up to the boil, reduce the heat and simmer for 4–5 minutes, stirring occasionally. Add in your chosen flavour combination and stir to combine. Place into serving bowls end enjoy.

SLOW COOKER METHOD:

1 For whichever version you're making, place all the ingredients in a heatproof bowl that fits inside your slow cooker. Create a water bath by filling the slow cooker with water until it reaches three-quarters of the way up the outside of the bowl, then pop the lid on and cook on the low setting for 8 hours or overnight.

UNCOOKED METHOD:

1 Place the oats and half the quantity of milk into a container and cover with a lid. Refrigerate overnight. Stir in the remaining ingredients just before serving.

BREAKFAST SHAKSHUKA

This is my go-to recipe for a lazy Sunday morning. It's got everything you could want in a breakfast. I love spicy lamb merguez sausages, but if you can't find them, replace them with uncured chorizo sausages. By the time this is ready, the aromas wafting through the house will be making everyone ravenous. Bring this dish straight to the table with some griddled sourdough or flatbread for the family to tuck in to.

SERVES 4

200 g (7 oz) merguez or uncured
   chorizo sausage, cut into
   bite-sized pieces
1 tablespoon olive oil
1 onion, very finely diced
1 green pepper, diced
4 garlic cloves, crushed
1 heaped teaspoon paprika
1 teaspoon ground cumin
2 x 400 g (14 oz) cans of chopped
   tomatoes
1 heaped teaspoon caster sugar
4 free-range eggs
100 g (3½ oz) feta cheese
Small handful of fresh dill, picked
Salt and pepper
Griddled sourdough or flatbread,
   to serve

CONVENTIONAL METHOD

1 Fry the sausage in the oil in a large pan over a medium heat for 3–4 minutes until browned, then add the onion, green pepper and garlic and cook for a further 4–5 minutes. Add the paprika and cumin and cook for 1–2 minutes, then pour in the tomatoes. Bring up to a simmer, then cook over a low heat for 40 minutes, until slightly thickened. Towards the end of the cooking time, stir through the sugar and season with salt and pepper.

2 Make 4 wells in the tomato sauce, then crack an egg into each one. Cover the pan with a lid and cook for a further 8–10 minutes, until the whites of the eggs are set. Crumble over the feta, then sprinkle over the fresh dill and some freshly ground black pepper. Bring the pan straight to the table and serve with griddled sourdough or flatbread.

SLOW COOKER METHOD:

1 If you have time, brown the sausage in a frying pan for 3–4 minutes, then add the onion, green pepper and garlic and cook for a further 4–5 minutes. Place all the ingredients in your slow cooker except for the eggs, feta and dill. Add a pinch of salt and pepper and stir well. Pop the lid on and cook on the high setting for 3 hours.

2 Make 4 wells in the tomato sauce, then crack in the eggs, cover with the lid and cook for a further 15–20 minutes, until the whites are set. Crumble over the feta, then sprinkle over the fresh dill and some freshly ground black pepper. Serve with griddled sourdough or flatbread.

MEXICAN THREE BEAN TACO BOWL

Not all slow food recipes are for the winter months. This summery taco bowl is packed full of fresh flavours and goodness. You can use whatever beans you like, dried or even three-bean-mix cans. If using dried beans, remember to soak them overnight first.

SERVES 4

1–2 tablespoons olive oil
1 onion, diced
1 green pepper, cut into strips
4 garlic cloves, crushed
2 heaped tablespoons tomato purée
2 teaspoons smoked paprika
1 heaped teaspoon ground coriander
1 teaspoon ground cumin
1 x 400 g (14 oz) can of black beans,
    drained and rinsed
1 x 400 g (14 oz) can of red kidney
    beans, drained and rinsed
1 x 400 g (14 oz) can of cannellini beans,
    drained and rinsed
600 ml (20 fl oz) vegetable stock if using
    the conventional method or 300 ml
    (½ pint) if using the slow cooker
    method
Salt and pepper

Salsa:
200 g (7 oz) baby plum tomatoes,
    finely diced
1 small red onion, finely diced
2 tablespoons finely chopped fresh
    coriander, plus extra to serve
Juice of 1 lime
4 teaspoons olive oil

To serve:
2 wholemeal tortillas
Boiled rice
2 ripe avocados, halved, pitted
    and diced
Soured cream

CONVENTIONAL METHOD

1 Heat the oil in a large frying pan over a medium heat. Add the onion, green pepper and garlic and cook for 5 minutes. Add the tomato purée, paprika, ground coriander and cumin and cook for 1 minute, then add the beans and 600 ml (20 fl oz) of stock. Season with salt and pepper and bring up to a simmer. Cover with a lid and cook on a low heat for 1–2 hours. This will allow the flavours to develop. If you desire a thicker sauce, remove the lid and simmer over a medium heat until thickened. Adjust the seasoning to taste.

2 Preheat the oven to 190°C (375°F), Gas Mark 5.

3 To make the salsa, place the tomatoes, onion and coriander in a bowl, then dress with the lime juice and olive oil. Season with a pinch of salt and pepper.

4 Cut each tortilla into rough triangles, then spread onto a baking tray. Cook in the oven for 10 minutes, until golden.

5 Serve the bean stew spooned on top of some boiled rice with the baked tortilla chips, salsa, diced avocado, a dollop of soured cream and some chopped fresh coriander.

SLOW COOKER METHOD

1 Heat the oil in a large frying pan over a medium heat. Add the onion, green pepper and garlic and cook for 5 minutes. Add the tomato purée, paprika, ground coriander and cumin and cook for 1 minute, then transfer to your slow cooker along with the beans and 300 ml (½ pint) of stock. Season with salt and pepper, then cover and cook on the low setting for 4 hours.

2 Follow steps 2–5 as above.

STEPH'S SPANISH CHICKEN

The first one in my family to be sold on the merits of using a slow cooker was my sister, Steph. With two young kids running around and with both her and her husband, Chaz, working long hours, she often preached the benefits of thinking ahead and popping on a recipe to tick away while at work. This Spanish chicken is one of her staples and it's fab, so I took it upon myself to steal the recipe from her. Cheers, Steph!

SERVES 4

1–2 tablespoons olive oil

4 skinless chicken thighs, approx. 500 g (1 lb 2 oz), bone in

2 onions, sliced

100 g (3½ oz) chorizo sausage, cubed

3 garlic cloves, crushed

4–5 thyme sprigs, leaves picked

1 heaped teaspoon smoked paprika

1 x 400 g (14 oz) can of chopped tomatoes

500 ml (18 fl oz) chicken stock if using the conventional method or 200 ml (⅓ pint) boiling chicken stock if using the slow cooker method

100 g (3½ oz) green olives, pitted

1 red pepper, diced

1 green pepper, diced

1 teaspoon caster sugar (or to taste)

2 tablespoons chopped flat leaf parsley

Salt and pepper

Boiled rice or sauté potatoes, to serve

CONVENTIONAL METHOD

1 Heat the oil in a large heavy-based casserole over a medium to high heat. Add the chicken thighs and cook until golden – this will take 3–4 minutes. Remove from the casserole and set aside.

2 In the same pot, fry the onions in a dash more oil for 5 minutes, then add the chorizo and garlic and cook for a further few minutes. (Skip frying the onions and garlic if you're using the Time Saver Garlic Base.) Stir in the thyme and paprika, then pour in the chopped tomatoes and 500 ml (18 fl oz) of stock. Bring up to a simmer, then add the chicken back in, cover and cook over a very low heat for 2 hours.

3 Add the olives and red and green peppers and cook for a further 10 minutes. Stir in the sugar to taste, then add the parsley, saving some for garnish, and season with salt and pepper before serving with boiled rice or sauté potatoes.

SLOW COOKER METHOD

1 Heat the oil in a large heavy-based pan over a medium heat. Add the chicken thighs and cook until golden – this will take 3–4 minutes. Put into your slow cooker along with the rest of the ingredients apart from the olives, sugar and parsley, making sure you use only 200 ml (⅓ pint) of boiling stock. Cook on the low setting for 7 hours.

2 Before serving, season with salt and pepper, then add the olives and sugar to taste. Finally, stir through the parsley, saving some for garnish, and serve with boiled rice or sauté potatoes.

TIME SAVER TIP
You could use 2 portions of the Time Saver Garlic Base on page 14 instead of the onions and garlic.

BRAZILIAN FISH STEW

This tropical fish stew from Brazil goes by the traditional name of *moqueca*. It has both creamy and spicy notes but is still light and fresh. You can use any fish you like. I always look to see what's freshest, but I love sea bass, monkfish, mullet, salmon or even squid along with the prawns. This stew is great on its own, but I enjoy some fluffy rice on the side to absorb the delicious sauce.

SERVES 4

2 tablespoons olive oil, plus extra for cooking
1 large onion, diced
1 fennel bulb, finely diced
1 green chilli, deseeded and chopped
1 red pepper, diced
1 green pepper, diced
3 garlic cloves, crushed
1 x 400 g (14 oz) can of chopped tomatoes
1 x 400 ml (14 fl oz) can of coconut milk
200 ml (⅓ pint) vegetable stock
5–6 splashes of hot sauce (or more to taste)
400 g (14 oz) fish fillets, cut into even-sized chunks
165 g (5¾ oz) raw prawns
Juice of 1 lime
Salt and pepper

To serve:
6 spring onions, sliced
Fresh coriander
Lime wedges
Boiled rice

CONVENTIONAL METHOD

1 Heat a splash of oil in a large pan over a medium heat. Add the onion, fennel and chilli and fry for 5 minutes, until softened. Add the red and green peppers and garlic and cook for a further 3 minutes. Pour in the tomatoes, coconut milk and stock and bring up to a simmer, then cook over the lowest possible heat for 40 minutes. At this point, add the hot sauce to taste.

2 Meanwhile, place the fish fillets and prawns in a bowl and marinate them in the lime juice and 2 tablespoons of olive oil for 20 minutes. Add the fish and prawns to the pan after the cooking time has elapsed and gently cook for 10 minutes. Season with salt and pepper.

3 Serve in bowls garnished with the spring onions and coriander. Add a lime wedge and a little more hot sauce if you like a kick. This stew can be enjoyed with a side of rice.

SLOW COOKER METHOD

1 Heat a splash of oil in a large pan over a medium heat. Add the onion, fennel and chilli and fry for 5 minutes, until softened. Add the garlic and cook for a further minute. Transfer to your slow cooker along with the red and green peppers, tomatoes, coconut milk and stock. Put on the lid and cook on the high setting for 2 hours.

2 Meanwhile, place the fish fillets and prawns in a bowl and marinate them in the lime juice and 2 tablespoons of olive oil for 20 minutes.

3 Turn the heat setting to high. Add the fish and prawns, stir well and cook for a further 10 minutes. Season with salt and pepper and the hot sauce, to taste.

4 Follow step 3 as for the conventional method opposite.

TIP

Make sure the fish is cut into the same size chunks so that they cook through at the same rate.

ROASTED BUTTERNUT SQUASH TAGINE

A North African tagine usually includes lamb, but what I love about the complex flavour profile is the sweetness that comes from the fruit, usually apricots, that's used to balance the spice. Using naturally sweet butternut squash or even sweet potatoes instead of meat makes this recipe not only economical, but delicious too. I always serve this with herby couscous and some natural yogurt with some harissa stirred through.

SERVES 4

1 large butternut squash, peeled and diced
1–2 tablespoons olive oil
1 large onion, finely chopped
5 garlic cloves, crushed
1 thumb-sized piece of fresh root ginger, finely chopped or grated
1 teaspoon smoked paprika
1 teaspoon ground cinnamon
1 teaspoon ground coriander
1 heaped teaspoon harissa paste
1 tablespoon tomato purée
1 x 500 g (1 lb 2 oz) carton of tomato passata
1 x 400 g (14 oz) can of chickpeas, drained and rinsed
100 g (3½ oz) dried apricots, finely chopped
200 ml (⅓ pint) vegetable stock
1 tablespoon honey (or to taste)
Salt and pepper

To serve:
Herby couscous
Natural yogurt spiked with harissa

CONVENTIONAL METHOD

1 Preheat the oven to 180°C (350°F), Gas Mark 4.
2 Place the squash in a bowl, drizzle with some oil and season with salt and pepper. Scatter onto a baking tray and roast in the oven for 30 minutes.
3 Meanwhile, heat a little more oil in a heavy-based pan over a low to medium heat. Add the onion, garlic and ginger and fry for 7–8 minutes, until softened. Add the spices and harissa and cook for a further 1–2 minutes. Stir in the tomato purée, then add the passata, chickpeas, apricots, stock and roasted squash, stirring to combine. Put on a lid, then simmer over the lowest heat for 1 hour. Add the honey to taste and season with salt and pepper.
4 Serve with herby couscous and a dollop of natural yogurt that has been spiked with harissa.

SLOW COOKER METHOD

1 If time allows, follow steps 1–2 as above to add bags of flavour.
2 Add all the ingredients apart from the honey to your slow cooker and season with salt and pepper. Add the butternut squash and stir to combine. Put the lid on and cook on the low setting for 6 hours or for 4 hours on high. Add the honey to taste.
3 Follow step 4 as above.

MINESTRONE WITH PISTOU

I have vivid memories of eating cans of minestrone soup round my Nanny Jack's as a kid. I actually used to enjoy it, but it didn't taste anything like this – it's not even in the same ball park. This is a combination of cultures, my take on Italian minestrone and a *pistou*, which is a French version of pesto that doesn't include the traditional pine nuts and Parmesan cheese. This is a great-tasting soup just as it is, but once you stir through that punchy *pistou* and cheese, it's a world away from the canned version I ate as a kid.

SERVES 4

1–2 tablespoons olive oil
1 onion, diced
1 large carrot, cut into small dice
2 celery sticks, cut into small dice
1 garlic clove, crushed
3 thyme sprigs
1 bay leaf
2 tablespoons tomato purée
1 x 400 g (14 oz) can of chopped
    tomatoes
1 x 400 g (14 oz) can of cannellini
    beans, drained and rinsed
1 litre (1¾ pints) chicken or vegetable
    stock
100 g (3½ oz) spaghetti, broken into
    small pieces
Salt and pepper
Parmesan cheese, for grating

Pistou:
Large bunch of basil
½ garlic clove
4 tablespoons extra virgin olive oil
Lemon juice, to taste

CONVENTIONAL METHOD

1 Heat the oil in a large heavy-based casserole over a medium heat. Add the onion, carrot and celery and gently fry for 5 minutes. Add the garlic, herbs and tomato purée and cook for 2 minutes. Pour in the tomatoes, beans and stock, season with salt and pepper, then pop on a lid and simmer for 40 minutes. Stir in the pasta and cook, uncovered, for a further 15 minutes.
2 To make the pistou, place the basil in a mini blender along with the garlic, olive oil and lemon juice to taste, then blend until you have a loose consistency. Season to taste with salt and pepper.
3 Serve the soup in bowls and dot on some of the pistou, then grate over some Parmesan.

SLOW COOKER METHOD

1 Pop all the ingredients apart from the pasta into your slow cooker and cook on the low setting for 6 hours.
2 Add the pasta and cook for a further 30 minutes. Season with salt and pepper.
3 Follow steps 2–3 as above.

MISO CHICKEN RAMEN

This is my go-to pick-me-up recipe because I just love the complexity of the flavours. Now before I get a hard time for mixing cuisines and ingredients, hear me out. I know that the sambal udang chilli paste should be nowhere near this dish, but I had some knocking around in the refrigerator when I was making this and loved the smoky heat it added. I think this prawn and chilli based condiment is worth searching for, it has a really savoury or umami flavour, and is also great in stir fries, fried rice and with vegetables. You can of course leave it out if you'd rather. Try this recipe with prawns, vegetables, tofu – there are so many possibilities.

SERVES 4

1–2 tablespoons olive oil

1.2 litres (2 pints) good-quality chicken or pork stock

300 ml (½ pint) soya milk

4 boneless, skinless chicken thighs, cut into bite-sized pieces

100 g (3½ oz) shiitake mushrooms, trimmed and sliced

1 x 260 g (9¼ oz) pack of ramen noodles

Miso base:

6 spring onions, white parts only, thinly sliced (reserve the green tops for garnish if you like)

3 garlic cloves, chopped

1 thumb-sized piece of fresh root ginger, chopped

50 ml (2 fl oz) mirin

2 tablespoons miso paste

1 tablespoon caster sugar

1 teaspoon sambal udang chilli paste, or 1 teaspoon dried red chilli flakes

To garnish:

Fresh coriander

1 spring onion, thinly sliced

1 red chilli, finely sliced

4 eggs, soft-boiled and halved

CONVENTIONAL METHOD

1 Pop all the miso base ingredients into a mini blender and blitz until smooth.

2 Heat the oil in a large heavy-based casserole, then add the miso base and cook over a low heat for 5 minutes. Pour in the stock and soya milk and bring up to a gentle simmer. Add the chicken and mushrooms, then cover and cook over the lowest heat possible for 2 hours.

3 Cook the noodles in boiling water for 4–5 minutes or according to the packet instructions, then portion into four bowls. Ladle over the chicken and miso broth, then garnish with fresh coriander leaves, spring onion, chilli and a soft-boiled egg.

SLOW COOKER METHOD

1 Pop all the miso base ingredients into a mini blender and blitz until smooth, then spoon into the slow cooker. Pour in the stock and soya milk and mix well. Add the chicken and mushrooms. Cover with the lid and cook on the low setting for 5 hours.

2 Follow step 3 as above.

SOUTH AFRICAN TUNA BREYANI ('FISH FOOD')

There's a funny story behind this recipe. My nan is from South Africa and this is one of the recipes she brought with her when she came to the UK, all of which became firm family favourites. My granddad, Les, thought the Cape Malay recipes such as *bredie* and *breyani* sounded a bit too exotic, so he renamed them 'tomato food' and 'fish food' and these are the names we know them by to this day in my household. This recipe doesn't look that mouth watering to the eye, but trust me on this one, it tastes incredible so please try it. I like to serve it with rice, pickled jalapeños and a good splash of Tabasco sauce.

SERVES 4

2 onions, finely diced

30 g (1 oz) butter

1 tablespoon olive oil

5 garlic cloves, crushed

1 heaped teaspoon ground cumin

1 teaspoon hot chilli powder

800 g (1 lb 12 oz) Maris Piper potatoes, cut into large cubes

700 ml (1¼ pints) chicken stock if using the conventional method or 400 ml (14 fl oz) if using the slow cooker method

2 x 160 g (5¾ oz) cans of tuna in spring water, drained

Salt and pepper

To serve:
Boiled rice
Pickled jalapeños
Tabasco sauce

CONVENTIONAL METHOD

1 Cook the onions in the butter and oil in a large heavy-based casserole set over a low to medium heat for 10 minutes, stirring frequently. Add the garlic and spices and cook for a further 2 minutes. Add the potatoes and give them a good stir before pouring in the stock and bringing up to a simmer – add enough stock to just cover the potatoes. Add the tuna, then cover and cook for around 1½ hours, until the potatoes are cooked through. Season well with salt and pepper. If you want a thicker consistency, remove the lid and simmer over a medium heat for 10 minutes at the end.

2 Serve with boiled rice, pickled jalapeños and a splash of Tabasco sauce if you like a kick of heat.

SLOW COOKER METHOD

1 Cook the onions in the butter and oil in a large pan set over a low to medium heat for 10 minutes, stirring frequently. Add the garlic and spices and cook for a further 2 minutes. Pop into your slow cooker along with the potatoes and tuna, then pour in the 400 ml (14 fl oz) of stock. Give it all a good stir, then cover with the lid and cook on the low setting for 7 hours. Season well with salt and pepper.
2 Follow step 2 as for the conventional method opposite.

COCONUT FISH CURRY

I get a great feeling of contentment when I'm making something from scratch, like this green curry paste. You can of course use a good-quality shop-bought paste, but sometimes the process makes the food taste even better. You can find kaffir lime leaves and shrimp paste in some supermarkets, but definitely in your local Asian market, plus everything is cheaper there too, from curry pastes and herbs to soy and sweet chilli sauce. Go check out some of the interesting ingredients on offer.

SERVES 4

2 x 400 ml (14 fl oz) cans of coconut milk
1 stick of lemongrass, bruised
1–2 tablespoons fish sauce, to taste
400 g (14 oz) monkfish, cut into chunks
200 g (7 oz) raw prawns
150 g (5½ oz) sugar-snap peas
Juice of 1 lime
1 tablespoon brown sugar or honey

Green curry paste:
5 garlic cloves, chopped
3 shallots, chopped
3 kaffir lime leaves, finely shredded
2 green chillies, deseeded and roughly chopped
1 thumb-sized piece of fresh root ginger, chopped
Stems from a small bunch of fresh coriander
1 heaped teaspoon shrimp paste
1 teaspoon ground coriander
½ teaspoon ground cumin

To serve:
Fresh coriander
1 red chilli, deseeded and thinly sliced
Boiled rice

CONVENTIONAL METHOD

1 Place all the ingredients for the curry paste in a mini blender or pestle and mortar and blitz or grind to a fine paste.
2 Carefully open the cans of coconut milk without shaking them and scoop off the coconut milk solids on the top. Reserve the liquid part of the coconut milk for later. Put the solids in a large pan over a medium heat, then add the curry paste and lemon grass and fry for 3–4 minutes.
3 Pour in the coconut milk liquid and fish sauce and bring up to a gentle simmer, then cover and cook for 40 minutes. Add the monkfish, prawns and sugar-snap peas and cook for a further 5 minutes, until the prawns are pink and the fish is cooked through. Add lime juice to taste and the brown sugar or honey. Remove and discard the lemon grass.
4 Garnish with fresh coriander leaves and sliced chilli and serve with rice.

SLOW COOKER METHOD:

1 Follow steps 1–2 as above, then add to your slow cooker along with the coconut milk liquid and fish sauce. Cover with the lid and cook on the low setting for 4 hours.
2 Pop the monkfish, prawns and sugar-snap peas in and cook on the high setting for 10 minutes, until the fish and prawns are cooked through. Add the lime juice to taste and the brown sugar or honey. Remove and discard the lemon grass.
3 Follow step 4 as above.

WARMING CARROT AND ORANGE SOUP

Would you believe that if carrots are cooked in a certain way, they actually taste of carrot? So many times we opt to boil carrots to within an inch of their life. There's a reason the water turns orange, and that's because all the flavour has leached out. If you cook them as in the recipe below, I guarantee you'll have the most flavour-packed carrots you've ever tried. I love to blitz them to make this soup and the addition of the crème fraîche really cuts through the sweetness.

SERVES 4

50 g (1¾ oz) unsalted butter
800 g (1 lb 12 oz) carrots, cut into
   2.5 cm (1 inch) chunks
1 onion, roughly chopped
2 garlic cloves, crushed
1 tablespoon grated fresh root
   ginger
Juice of 1 large orange
600 ml (20 fl oz) vegetable stock if
   using the conventional method or
   300 ml (½ pint) boiling vegetable
   stock if using the slow cooker
   method
100 ml (3½ fl oz) crème fraîche
Salt and pepper

To serve:
100 g (3½ oz) feta cheese, crumbled
2 tablespoons extra virgin olive oil,
   for drizzling

CONVENTIONAL METHOD

1 Melt the butter in a saucepan over a medium heat, then add the carrots, onion, garlic and ginger and season with salt and pepper. Pour in the orange juice, then cover tightly with a lid. You may want to use a sheet of foil too to make sure none of the steam escapes. Lower the heat to its lowest setting, then cook for 40–45 minutes until tender, giving the pan a gentle shake now and then to make sure the veg are not catching on the bottom.

2 Pour in the 600 ml (20 fl oz) of stock and bring to a simmer. Take off the heat and use a stick blender or food processor to whizz until smooth and silky, then stir through the crème fraîche and season with salt and pepper.

3 Ladle into bowls, then crumble over the feta and finally drizzle over the extra virgin olive oil.

SLOW COOKER METHOD

1 Pop the butter and orange juice into your slow cooker, then scatter in the carrots, onion, garlic and ginger and season with salt and pepper. Put on your lid and cook on the low setting for 6 hours.

2 Spoon into a suitable vessel, then pour in the 300 ml (½ pint) of boiling stock. Use a stick blender or food processor to whizz until smooth and silky. Finally, stir through the crème fraîche and season with salt and pepper.

3 Follow step 3 as above.

GREEK BEAN STEW

This is such a light and simple recipe, perfect for the summer months. It's also great for an occasion like a barbecue when you have other elements on the go. You can dump everything in the pot and let it do its thing, but cooking the onions first until they are sweet and delicious takes this stew to a new level. I like to serve this with an additional drizzle of olive oil and some steaming pitta breads.

SERVES 4

1–2 tablespoons olive oil
2 onions, diced
3 celery sticks, finely diced
3 garlic cloves, crushed
1 heaped tablespoon tomato purée
½ teaspoon paprika
2 x 400 g (14 oz) cans of butter beans, drained and rinsed
1 x 400 g (14 oz) can of chopped tomatoes
500 ml (18 fl oz) vegetable stock if using the conventional method or 300 ml (½ pint) if using the slow cooker method
Pinch of caster sugar
Salt and pepper

To serve:
100 g (3½ oz) feta cheese, crumbled
Flat leaf parsley
Extra virgin olive oil, for drizzling
Pitta bread

CONVENTIONAL METHOD

1 Heat the oil in a large pan over a low heat. Add the onions, celery and garlic. Fry for 10 minutes, until golden and softened. Stir through the tomato purée and paprika and cook for a further minute.
2 Add the beans, tomatoes and 500 ml (18 fl oz) of stock, then season with a good pinch of salt and pepper. Cover and cook over a low heat for 1 hour. Add the sugar.
3 Ladle into bowls, then scatter over the crumbled feta and garnish with parsley before drizzling with a little extra virgin olive oil. Serve with warm pitta bread on the side.

SLOW COOKER METHOD

1 Follow step 1 as above, then pop all the ingredients into your slow cooker except the sugar, feta and parsley, making sure you use only 300 ml (½ pint) of stock. Season with salt and pepper, then cover and cook on the low setting for 7 hours. Add the sugar.
2 Follow step 3 as above.

ROY'S FAMOUS OFF-THE-MENU HOT WINGS

After I started going to his restaurant on a regular basis (too regular for my bank balance), I struck up a great friendship with my pal Rohim. He and his brothers have always looked after my family and me over the years, even inviting us to enjoy Iftar with them. Roy always goes the extra mile and makes me these incredible sticky wings, even though they're not on the menu. Like most people I don't have a tandoor at home, so I've devised this recipe to try to recreate the hot, sweet and flavour-packed chicken wings served to me in Roy's curry house.

SERVES 4

1 kg (2 lb 4 oz) chicken wings
  (around 12 whole wings)
1 teaspoon garlic powder
1 teaspoon smoked paprika
1 teaspoon garam masala
Pinch of salt
2 tablespoons chopped fresh
  coriander, to garnish

Sticky glaze:
1–2 tablespoons olive oil
2 garlic cloves, crushed
1 red chilli, deseeded and chopped
Juice of ½ lime, plus extra for serving
4 tablespoons sweet chilli sauce
2 tablespoons soy sauce

CONVENTIONAL METHOD

1 Preheat the oven to 180°C (350°F), Gas Mark 4.
2 Cut off and discard the wing tips, then cut each wing at the joint to make two pieces. Pop the wings into a bowl, sprinkle in all the spices and a pinch of salt and mix well.
3 Place the wings on a wire rack set over a baking tray (line the tray with foil for a much easier clean-up) and cook in the oven for 30 minutes. Crank the heat up to 200°C (400°F), Gas Mark 6 and cook for a further 20 minutes, until golden and crispy.
4 To make the glaze, heat the oil in a large pan over a medium heat. Pop the garlic and chilli in the pan and fry for 30 seconds. Add the lime juice, sweet chilli sauce and soy sauce. Place the cooked wings in the pan and toss to coat with the glaze. Finally, sprinkle with the fresh coriander and serve with the remaining half a lime for squeezing over.

SLOW COOKER METHOD

1 Follow step 2 as above.
2 Place the chicken wings in the slow cooker along with a small splash of water, put on the lid and cook on the low setting for 4 hours or on high for 2 hours. Use a slotted spoon to remove the wings from the slow cooker.
3 Follow step 4 as above.

TIP

If time allows, I like to pop the cooked slow cooker wings into a hot oven for 5–10 minutes to crisp them up before glazing them in the sauce.

Comfort Food

Comfort food doesn't always equate to heavy recipes suited to the chilly winter months. This chapter showcases some of my favourite recipes, from Braised Faggots in Rich Cider Gravy and the American classic of slow-cooked Barbecue Pulled Pork to a zesty, spicy Pork Belly Bahn Mi sandwich.

For me, comfort food also means seeing people enjoying themselves. There is no better feeling than seeing someone tucking in to my food and wanting more. I love it when Indie turns round to me after school and asks for her Must-Have Shepherd's Pie – rich, filling and with a cheesy mash on top, always with broccoli on the side and lashings of gravy, no more and no less.

Whatever the occasion and whatever the time of year, these recipes provide comfort when you most need it.

LOW AND SLOW BEEF RENDANG

This is one of my favourite curries – a hot, highly fragrant, salty, sweet and sour treat to replace your weekend takeaway. The beef cooks slowly until really tender, then almost fries in the oil left by the coconut milk to form a crust on the meat. Kecap manis is a sweet Indonesian soy sauce that adds a wonderful saltiness and sweetness to the recipe. You can find it in most supermarkets, but if not, use a good-quality soy sauce and add sugar to taste.

SERVES 4

1–2 tablespoons olive oil

800 g (1 lb 12 oz) skirt steak, cut into
2.5 cm (1 inch) cubes

2 tablespoons plain flour seasoned
with salt and pepper

2 onions, finely diced

3 garlic cloves, crushed

2 large sticks of lemongrass, cut in half
lengthways and bruised

1 large red chilli, deseeded and diced

1 thumb-sized piece of fresh root
ginger, grated

1 x 140 g (5 oz) can of tomato purée

1 heaped tablespoon garam masala

1 teaspoon paprika

½ teaspoon ground turmeric

½ teaspoon ground cinnamon

1 tablespoon brown sugar or palm sugar

1 x 400 ml (14 fl oz) can of coconut milk

400 ml (14 fl oz) boiling beef stock if
using the conventional method or
200 ml (⅓ pint) if using the slow
cooker method

3 tablespoons kecap manis or soy
sauce with sugar to taste

Juice of 1 lime

Fresh coriander, to garnish

Boiled rice, to serve

CONVENTIONAL METHOD

1 Preheat the oven to 150°C (300°F), Gas Mark 2.

2 Heat the oil in a large heavy-based casserole over a medium to high heat. Dust the cubed beef in the flour, then add to the casserole and sear for 5–6 minutes, until golden. Remove from the pot and set aside. You may have to do this in batches so that you don't overcrowd the pot. Add the onions, garlic, lemongrass, chilli and ginger and fry for 5 minutes, until golden. (Or you could use the Time Saver Curry Base instead of the onions, garlic and ginger called for here.)

3 Stir in the tomato purée, spices and sugar, then pour in the coconut milk and 400 ml (14 fl oz) of stock. Bring to a gentle simmer, then return the beef to the casserole. Put on a tight-fitting lid and cook in the oven for 4 hours. The sauce should be thick, rich and coating the beef. If not, remove the lid and reduce the sauce for a few minutes over a medium heat on the hob. Season with the kecap manis and a good squeeze of lime juice.

4 Remove the lemongrass stalks before garnishing with fresh coriander. Serve with a side of rice.

SLOW COOKER METHOD

1 Follow step 2 as above.

2 Transfer the onion mixture to your slow cooker, then add the tomato purée, spices, sugar, coconut milk and 200 ml (⅓ pint) of stock. Stir well, then add the beef. Cover with the lid and cook on the low setting for 7 hours.

3 Pull the lid slightly ajar and cook on the high setting for a further 30 minutes. Transfer everything to a large frying pan and reduce the sauce for a few minutes over a medium heat on the hob. Season with the kecap manis and a good squeeze of lime juice.

4 Follow step 4 as above.

TIME SAVER TIP
You could use 2 portions of the Time Saver Curry Base on page 14 instead of the onions, garlic and ginger.

STEPH'S CHEAT'S HUNTER'S CHICKEN

My lovely sister Steph's version of a pub classic, hunter's chicken, uses chicken breasts (although you could use thighs if you'd rather) wrapped in bacon, cooked slowly in an unctuous, sticky barbecue sauce, then topped with melted Mexicana Cheddar cheese (normal Cheddar is fine if you don't like chilli heat). Steph often uses a jar of shop-bought barbecue sauce in her slow cooker to speed things up. There's nothing wrong with a cheat here and there, but it isn't a patch on my homemade version, which not only tastes incredible, but you can control what's in it. No excuses next time, Steph!

SERVES 4

4 skinless, boneless chicken breasts
½ pack halloumi cheese, approx.
    115 g (4 oz), sliced into 4 batons
12 streaky bacon rashers
100 g (3½ oz) Mexicana Cheddar
    cheese, grated

Barbecue sauce:
1–2 tablespoons olive oil
1 onion, very finely chopped or
    thinly sliced
2 garlic cloves, crushed
150 ml (¼ pint) tomato ketchup
40 ml (1½ fl oz) cider vinegar
3 tablespoons Worcestershire sauce
2 tablespoons honey
1 tablespoon soy sauce
1 teaspoon English mustard
½ teaspoon smoked paprika

CONVENTIONAL METHOD

1 Preheat the oven to 180°C (350°F), Gas Mark 4.
2 To make the barbecue sauce, heat the oil in a pan over a medium heat. Add the onion and garlic and cook for 5 minutes. Add all the other ingredients and bring up to the boil. Remove from the heat and set aside.
3 Cut a pocket into each chicken breast and place a piece of halloumi inside. Wrap each breast in 3 slices of bacon, then pop into a baking dish, pour over the barbecue sauce and cover the dish with foil.
4 Cook in the oven for 30 minutes. Remove from the oven and take off the foil, then sprinkle over the grated cheese and pop back in the oven, uncovered, for 10–15 minutes, until the cheese has melted and the chicken is cooked through.

SLOW COOKER METHOD

1 Put all the barbecue sauce ingredients in the slow cooker and mix well. I prefer sliced onions in the slow cooker because it creates a base for the chicken and protects it from the direct heat of the pot.
2 Cut a pocket into each chicken breast and place a piece of halloumi inside. Wrap each breast in 3 slices of bacon, then pop into the slow cooker and baste with the sauce. Cover with the lid and cook on the low setting for 6 hours.
3 To finish, baste the chicken again, then sprinkle over the cheese and cook until it has melted.

BARBECUE PULLED PORK

No self-respecting slow food cookbook should be without a pulled pork recipe. There's a reason why this dish in particular took off worldwide – it's absolutely delicious! The dry rub is key to build layers of flavour. You can put a few drops of liquid smoke (available online) in your cooking liquid to add an additional smoky note to the pork, but it's not essential.

SERVES 4–6

2 kg (4 lb 8 oz) pork shoulder, bone in the neck end if you can get it, rind removed
1 onion, sliced
200 ml (⅓ pint) dry cider
200 ml (⅓ pint) chicken stock
40 ml (1½ fl oz) cider vinegar
2–3 drops of liquid smoke, to taste (optional)
Salt and pepper

Dry rub:
2 tablespoons soft brown sugar
1 tablespoon dried thyme
1 tablespoon ground fennel seeds
1 heaped teaspoon smoked paprika
1 teaspoon garlic powder
1 teaspoon onion powder
1 teaspoon ground black pepper
1 teaspoon salt

To serve:
Brioche burger buns
Slaw

CONVENTIONAL METHOD

1 Mix together all the dry rub ingredients, then rub very well into the pork. Cover and marinate in the refrigerator for 24 hours.
2 The next day, preheat the oven to 230°C (450°F), Gas Mark 8.
3 Place the sliced onion in the bottom of a large roasting tin, then place the pork on top and pour in the cider, stock, vinegar and liquid smoke (if using), being careful not to wash off the dry rub.
4 Roast in the oven, uncovered, for 20 minutes. Remove from the oven and cover tightly with a sheet of foil, then turn the heat down to 140°C (275°F), Gas Mark 1 and roast for a further 6 hours. Uncover the tray and give it a final 15 minutes at 230°C (450°F), Gas Mark 8.
5 Once cooked, remove from the oven and leave to rest in the tray for 30 minutes. Pull the pork apart using forks, then leave to rest in the cooking juices so they can be reabsorbed into the shredded pork. Season to taste with salt and pepper.
6 Serve the pulled pork in the brioche buns with some slaw on the side.

SLOW COOKER METHOD

1 Follow step 1 as above.
2 Place the sliced onion in the bottom of the slow cooker, then place the pork on top and pour in the cider, stock, vinegar and liquid smoke (if using), being careful not to wash off the dry rub. Cover and cook on the high setting for 5–6 hours or the low setting for 8–9 hours.
3 Remove the pork from the pot and pull it apart using forks. Place the shredded pork in a bowl and add enough of the cooking juices to moisten it. Season with salt and pepper.
4 Follow step 6 as above.

ANGELA'S WELSH LAMB CAWL

I studied in Wales for a couple of years and at one point I had a lovely landlady named Angela. On occasion she used to kindly cook for us 18-year-old lads and she introduced me to delicious Welsh cawl, a beautiful slow-cooked stew. The salty cheese dropped in at the last minute was a revelation and we used to mop up the juices with loads of fresh crusty bread. I love this with the inexpensive scrag end of lamb on the bone because it adds loads of flavour, but lamb neck fillets work great too. You will also find scrag end in a lot of the lamb stewing packs in your supermarket.

SERVES 4

1 kg (2 lb 4 oz) scrag end of lamb (get your butcher to cut it into 2–3 pieces)

2 tablespoons plain flour seasoned with salt and pepper

1–2 tablespoons olive oil

1 onion, sliced

2 small leeks, sliced (keep the green and white parts separate)

2 carrots, cut into chunks

250 g (9 oz) swede, cut into small chunks

200 g (7 oz) Maris Piper potatoes, cut into chunks

2 rosemary sprigs

1 bay leaf

850 ml (1½ pints) lamb stock if using the conventional method or 500 ml (18 fl oz) if using the slow cooker method

¼ head of Savoy cabbage, shredded

Salt and pepper

To serve:

150 g (5½ oz) Caerphilly cheese, crumbled

Crusty bread

CONVENTIONAL METHOD

1 Place the lamb in a bowl and toss with the seasoned flour. Heat the oil in a large heavy-based casserole over a medium to high heat. Add the lamb and fry in batches for 5–6 minutes, until golden, then remove from the pot and set aside. Add the onion and the white part of the leeks and cook over a gentle heat for 5 minutes, until softened.

2 Return the lamb to the casserole along with the carrots, swede, potatoes, rosemary and bay leaf. Pour in the 850 ml (1½ pints) of stock and bring up to a simmer. Cover and cook over a gentle heat for 3 hours.

3 Remove the lamb from the pot and leave to cool before taking it off the bone and shredding the meat. Add the lamb back to the casserole along with the cabbage and the green part of the leeks. Cook for a further 10 minutes, uncovered. Remove the rosemary sprigs and bay leaf and season to taste with salt and pepper.

4 Ladle into bowls, then just before tucking in scatter in the crumbled Caerphilly and enjoy with some crusty bread.

SLOW COOKER METHOD

1 Follow step 1 as above.

2 Put the lamb mixture in your slow cooker along with the carrots, swede, potatoes, rosemary and bay leaf. Pour in the 500 ml (18 fl oz) of stock and season with salt and pepper. Put the lid on and cook on the low setting for 6 hours.

3 Remove the lamb from the slow cooker and leave to cool before taking it off the bone and shredding the meat. Add the lamb back to the slow cooker along with the cabbage and the green part of the leeks and cook on the low setting for a further 30 minutes. Remove the rosemary sprigs and bay leaf and season to taste with salt and pepper.

4 Follow step 4 as above.

PORK BELLY BAHN MI

Some people think slow-cooked recipes are only suitable for the colder gloomy months, but this really is a must-try recipe for any time of year. This bright and vibrant Vietnamese street-food sandwich punches above its weight in terms of flavour. The lightly pickled vegetables cut through the richness of the slow-roasted pork. I like to cook the pork the day before, then slice it when cool and crisp it up on both sides in a hot pan until golden.

SERVES 4

1.2 kg (2 lb 10 oz) pork belly, skin removed
400 ml (14 fl oz) water if using the conventional method or 150 ml (¼ pint) if using the slow cooker method
1 onion, sliced (slow cooker method only)
Salt and pepper

Pickle:
1 carrot, julienned
½ mooli, julienned
50 g (1¾ oz) caster sugar
100 ml (3½ fl oz) white wine vinegar or rice wine vinegar
1 teaspoon salt

To serve:
1 large baguette, cut into 4
150 g (5½ oz) pork liver pâté
3 tablespoons sriracha mayonnaise, or mix 1 part sriracha to 3 parts mayo
1 small chilli, thinly sliced (you can use red or green chillies or a mixture of both)
Small bunch of fresh coriander
50 g (1¾ oz) crushed salted peanuts

CONVENTIONAL METHOD

1 Preheat the oven to 150°C (300°F), Gas Mark 2.
2 Season the pork belly with salt and pepper, then place on a rack set inside a roasting tin. Pour in the 400 ml (14 fl oz) of water, then cover the tin with foil and roast in the oven for 4 hours.
3 If you're going to serve the pork now, remove it from the oven and crank up the heat to 220°C (425°F), Gas Mark 7. Take off the foil and cook for a further 20–25 minutes, until crisp and golden. Rest for at least 20 minutes before slicing. Alternatively, cook the pork the day before and chill before slicing and reheating in a hot dry frying pan (the pork will release its own fat when reheated) until it's crisp and golden.
4 Meanwhile, to make the pickle, place the carrot and mooli in a bowl along with the sugar, vinegar and salt and leave for 1 hour.
5 Halve the baguette pieces and spread the pâté on the bottom half. Add some of the sliced pork belly, then top with pickled carrot and mooli and drizzle over the sriracha mayo. Finally, scatter with some chilli, coriander leaves and crushed peanuts.

SLOW COOKER METHOD

1 Place the onion in the slow cooker, then place the pork belly on top. Pour in the 150 ml (¼ pint) of water and season with salt and pepper. Put the lid on and cook on the low setting for 7 hours.
2 Remove the pork from the slow cooker and leave to rest for 20 minutes before slicing. Alternatively, cook the pork the day before and chill before slicing and reheating in a hot dry pan until it's crisp and golden.
3 Follow steps 4–5 as above.

DUCK MASSAMAN CURRY

I really love this fragrant massaman curry. You can use chicken, pork, lamb or beef in this one, but I really like to use inexpensive duck legs, which along with the addition of the cashew nuts bring an amazing richness to this classic Thai recipe. You can find massaman curry paste in most major supermarkets, but if you can't get it, substitute it with a good-quality Thai red curry paste. You'll find that curry pastes vary in strength depending on the brand, so adjust the amount you use to taste.

SERVES 4

4 duck legs
1 x 400 ml (14 fl oz) can of coconut milk
60 g (2¼ oz) cashew nuts, toasted
2 onions, sliced
5 garlic cloves, crushed
1 thumb-sized piece of fresh root
    ginger, grated
1 stick of lemongrass, bruised
1 red chilli, deseeded and diced
3 tablespoons massaman or Thai red
    curry paste
1 cinnamon stick
1 star anise
1 heaped tablespoon garam masala
400 g (14 oz) waxy potatoes (such as
    Desiree), cut into 2.5 cm (1 inch)
    pieces
200 ml (⅓ pint) chicken stock
2–3 tablespoons fish sauce
1 heaped tablespoon dark brown
    sugar or palm sugar (or to taste)
Juice of 1 lime (or to taste)
Thai jasmine rice, to serve

CONVENTIONAL METHOD

1 Place the duck legs in a large heavy-based casserole and cook over a medium heat until golden. At this stage you are trying to render some of the fat from the duck. Remove the duck from the pan, then pour off and reserve most of the fat (perfect for making roast potatoes with on another day).

2 Pour half of the coconut milk into a blender and blitz with the toasted cashews until smooth.

3 Add the onions, garlic, ginger (or Time Saver Curry Base) and lemongrass to the casserole and cook over a medium heat for 5 minutes, until golden. Add the chilli and cook for a couple of minutes more. Add the curry paste and spices, then add the potatoes. Pour in the blended coconut milk and cashews along with the remaining coconut milk, stock and fish sauce to taste and bring to a simmer.

4 Pop the duck legs back into the casserole, put a lid on and cook over a low heat for 2 hours.

5 By the end of the cooking time the sauce should be thick, rich and coating the potatoes. If not, increase the heat and reduce the sauce, uncovered, for a few minutes. Add the sugar and lime juice to taste and serve with Thai jasmine rice.

TIME SAVER TIP
You could use 2 portions of the Time Saver Curry Base on page 14 instead of the onions, garlic and ginger.

SLOW COOKER METHOD

1 Follow steps 1–3 as for the conventional method opposite.
2 Transfer the contents of the pot to your slow cooker and pop the duck legs in on top. Put the lid on and cook on the low setting for 6 hours.
3 Add the sugar and lime juice to taste and serve with Thai jasmine rice.

MASALA BRAISED LAMB SHANKS

Lamb shanks have so often been seen as just a pub menu staple over the years, normally served in a sometimes nasty red wine sauce with the obligatory sprig of rosemary. My Indian-spiced shanks are the perfect recipe for both slow cooking and slow cookers. This is the sort of recipe that really got my creative juices going when writing this book. It's so simple – just put everything together and let the gentle heat create all the magic.

SERVES 4

1–2 tablespoons olive oil

4 small lamb shanks

1 onion, thinly sliced

4 garlic cloves, crushed

1 thumb-sized piece of fresh root ginger, grated

1 green chilli, deseeded and diced

2 heaped tablespoons tomato purée

2 tablespoons garam masala

1 teaspoon ground cinnamon

1 teaspoon mustard seeds

½ teaspoon ground turmeric

600 ml (20 fl oz) chicken stock if using the conventional method or 200 ml (⅓ pint) if using the slow cooker method

1 x 400 ml (14 fl oz) can of coconut milk

1 heaped tablespoon mango chutney

Salt and pepper

Basmati rice, to serve

To garnish:

Fresh coriander

Seeds from ½ pomegranate

CONVENTIONAL METHOD

1 Heat the oil in a large heavy-based casserole over a medium to high heat. Add the lamb shanks and seal all over for 7–8 minutes, until golden, then remove from the casserole and set aside. Add the onion, garlic, ginger (or Time Saver Curry Base) and chilli and cook over a medium heat for 5 minutes, until the onion is golden. Add the tomato purée and spices and cook for 1–2 minutes, then pour in the 600 ml (20 fl oz) of stock and the coconut milk.

2 Return the shanks to the casserole and bring up to a gentle simmer. Reduce the heat to its lowest setting, cover with a lid and cook gently for around 3 hours. When cooked, remove the shanks and reduce the liquid if required for a thicker sauce. Stir through the chutney and season with salt and pepper.

3 Serve the shanks with basmati rice and divide the sauce between the 4 servings. Finally, garnish with fresh coriander and pomegranate seeds.

SLOW COOKER METHOD

1 Follow step 1 as above, making sure you use only 200 ml (⅓ pint) of stock.

2 Place the shanks in your slow cooker, then pour over the coconut sauce. Put the lid on and cook on the low setting for 8 hours.

3 Gently remove the shanks, then stir through the chutney and season with salt and pepper.

4 Follow step 3 as above.

TIME SAVER TIP
You could use 1 portion of the Time Saver Curry Base on page 14 instead of the onion, garlic and ginger.

TURKEY CACCIATORE

I'm not sure why turkey meat isn't enjoyed at home in our family meals more often outside of the festive period. It's inexpensive, lean and very tasty. I'm using thigh meat in this recipe because it's more suitable for slow cooking, but you could also try breast or even chicken in this delicious Italian classic. I love to grate some Parmesan cheese on mine and I always serve it with pasta and a side of crusty garlic bread.

SERVES 4

1–2 tablespoons olive oil
400 g (14 oz) turkey thigh meat, diced
1 onion, diced
1 red pepper, diced
200 g (7 oz) mushrooms, trimmed
    and sliced
3 garlic cloves, crushed
150 ml (¼ pint) red wine
1 x 400 g (14 oz) can of chopped
    tomatoes
200 ml (⅓ pint) chicken stock if
    using the conventional method
    or 100 ml (3½ fl oz) if using the
    slow cooker method
1 tablespoon tomato purée
1 tablespoon dried oregano
1 tablespoon chopped rosemary
1 teaspoon chilli flakes (or to taste)
1 teaspoon cornflour (slow cooker
    method only)
1 tablespoon water (slow cooker
    method only)
1 teaspoon caster sugar (or to taste)
85g (3oz) black olives, pitted and
    halved
Salt and pepper

To serve:
Parmesan cheese, grated
Pasta
Garlic Tear 'n' Share Loaf (see
    page 166)

CONVENTIONAL METHOD

1 Heat the oil in a large heavy-based casserole over a medium to high heat. Add the diced turkey and fry for 5–6 minutes, until golden, then add the onion, red pepper, mushrooms and garlic and cook for 5 minutes. Pour in the wine and reduce by half, then stir through the chopped tomatoes, 200 ml (⅓ pint) of stock, tomato purée, oregano, rosemary and chilli flakes. Put on a lid and cook over a low heat for 1 hour. If you like a thicker sauce, then remove the lid at the end of the cooking time and simmer over a low to medium heat for a few minutes.

2 Before serving, season with salt and pepper and add sugar to taste. Stir through the olives, then grate over some Parmesan and serve with pasta and garlic bread.

SLOW COOKER METHOD

1 Put all the ingredients in your slow cooker apart from the cornflour, water, sugar and olives, making sure you use only 100 ml (3½ fl oz) of stock. Season with a pinch of salt and pepper and stir well. Pop on the lid and cook on the low setting for 7 hours.

2 Mix the cornflour and water together, then add to the slow cooker and stir well. Pop the lid back on and cook for a further 30 minutes.

3 Follow step 2 as above.

CREAMY CHICKEN AND TARRAGON CASSEROLE

When I was 16 years old I worked as a waiter at a large hotel in Bristol. This is where I got my first experience of fine dining, but it was one of the banqueting dishes, chicken in a creamy white wine and mushroom sauce, that stood out for me – it was just so tasty. This is my easy home-cooked version and you don't need a long list of ingredients. Browning the chicken and mushrooms will benefit you in the flavour stakes, especially if you're using a slow cooker. I love this served with champ.

SERVES 4

1–2 tablespoons olive oil

600 g (1 lb 5 oz) boneless, skinless chicken thighs, diced

200 g (7 oz) chestnut mushrooms, trimmed and sliced

1 onion, thinly sliced

3 garlic cloves, crushed

100 ml (3½ fl oz) white wine

400 ml (14 fl oz) chicken stock if using the conventional method or 200 ml (⅓ pint) boiling chicken stock if using the slow cooker method

50 ml (2 fl oz) double cream

Juice of ½ lemon

Small handful of tarragon leaves

Salt and pepper

Champ, to serve

CONVENTIONAL METHOD

1 Heat the oil in a large heavy-based casserole over a high heat. Add the chicken and cook for 2–3 minutes, then remove from the casserole and set aside. Pop in the mushrooms and cook until golden, which will take 6–7 minutes. Reduce to a medium heat. Add the onion and garlic and cook for a couple more minutes. Pour in the wine and reduce by half.

2 Pour in the 400 ml (14 fl oz) of stock, then add the chicken back in. Pop on a lid and simmer over a low heat for 40–50 minutes until the chicken is tender and cooked through.

3 Finish by pouring in the cream, squeezing in the lemon juice and seasoning with salt and pepper. Finally, stir through the tarragon and serve with champ.

SLOW COOKER METHOD

1 Follow step 1 as above.

2 Transfer the golden chicken and the mushroom mixture to your slow cooker along with the 200 ml (⅓ pint) of boiling stock and season with salt and pepper. Put the lid on and cook on the low setting for 6 hours.

3 Follow step 3 as above.

SMOKY LENTIL AND BEAN CHILLI

This is a vegetarian version of a classic chilli con carne. Puy lentils replace the minced beef in this one, but you won't miss the meat. The lentils not only add flavour, but also a great texture. This is a really healthy and inexpensive family meal that I like to serve with rice, grated cheese and some soured cream. Ready-to-eat lentils are available in most supermarkets and should be easy to find.

SERVES 4

1–2 tablespoons olive oil

1 large onion, diced

1 green pepper, finely diced

4 garlic cloves, crushed

1 heaped teaspoon ground cumin

1 heaped teaspoon dried oregano

1 teaspoon ground cinnamon

1 teaspoon smoked paprika

1 teaspoon chilli powder

1 tablespoon tomato purée

1 x 400 g (14 oz) can of red kidney
    beans, drained and rinsed

1 x 250 g (9 oz) pack of ready-to-eat
    Puy lentils

500 ml (18 fl oz) vegetable stock if
    using the conventional method or
    200 ml (⅓ pint) if using the slow
    cooker method

20 g (¾ oz) dark chocolate, at least
    70 per cent cocoa solids, broken
    into small chunks or grated

1 teaspoon caster sugar

Salt and pepper

Fresh coriander, to garnish (optional)

To serve:
Boiled rice
Grated Cheddar cheese
Soured cream

CONVENTIONAL METHOD

1 Heat the oil in a large heavy-based casserole over a medium heat. Add the onion, green pepper and garlic and fry for 3–4 minutes, then add the cumin, oregano, cinnamon, smoked paprika and chilli powder and cook for another 1–2 minutes. Stir in the tomato purée, then add the kidney beans, lentils and 500 ml (18 fl oz) of stock.

2 Cover and cook on a low heat for at least 2 hours. Towards the end of the cooking time, season with salt and pepper, then balance the chilli heat with the chocolate and sugar.

3 Ladle into bowls with some boiled rice and garnish with fresh coriander (if using). Serve with grated cheese and soured cream on the side.

SLOW COOKER METHOD

1 If time allows, follow step 1 as above before transferring to your slow cooker, as you will get a deeper flavour. However, if you're rushed for time, then put all the ingredients except the chocolate, sugar and coriander into your slow cooker, making sure you use only 200 ml (⅓ pint) of stock. Stir well and season with salt and pepper. Cover with the lid and cook on the low setting for 6 hours. At the end of the cooking time, balance the chilli heat with the chocolate and sugar.

2 Follow step 3 as above.

POTATO AND BACON 'PANAKETTY'

This was a weekly staple meal in the Edwards family growing up. A neighbour gave this recipe to my mum and we loved it! I've since found out that it was inspired by the Northern dish known as pan haggerty. It seems that something was lost in translation and so the Edwards 'panaketty' was born. As a growing boy this was filling and delicious and for my mum it was easy and economical. This is nothing like the original pan haggerty, but it's delicious in its own right and is my idea of comfort food.

SERVES 4

1 tablespoon olive oil

240 g (8½ oz) smoked streaky bacon rashers, cut into 2.5 cm (1 inch) pieces

1 kg (2 lb 4 oz) Maris Piper potatoes, cut into slices 5 mm (¼ inch) thick

2 onions, thinly sliced

1 tablespoon thyme leaves

800 ml (28 fl oz) chicken stock

40 g (1½ oz) butter, melted (conventional method only)

Salt and pepper

CONVENTIONAL METHOD

1 Preheat the oven to 160°C (325°F), Gas Mark 3.
2 Heat the oil in a casserole over a medium heat. Add the bacon and fry until golden, then remove from the pan and set aside.
3 Layer the potatoes, onions, bacon and a sprinkle of thyme leaves in the casserole and season with salt and pepper, then repeat until all the ingredients have been used up, finishing with a layer of potatoes. Gently pour in the stock, then put on a lid and cook in the oven for 3 hours.
4 Remove from the oven and brush the top layer of potatoes with the melted butter. Return to the oven, uncovered, for a further 30 minutes, until the potatoes are golden.

SLOW COOKER METHOD

1 Follow step 2 as above.
2 In your slow cooker, layer the potatoes, onions, bacon and a sprinkle of thyme leaves and season with salt and pepper, then repeat until all the ingredients have been used up, finishing with a layer of potatoes. Gently pour in the stock, then put on the lid and cook on the low setting for 7 hours.

INDIE'S MUST-HAVE SHEPHERD'S PIE

Shepherd's pie is my daughter Indie's ultimate all-time favourite dinner. She always has it with broccoli, but a big bowl of buttered peas are good too. When Indie is moaning that she's hungry, I use my secret kitchen weapon: shop-bought mashed potatoes. I've used lamb breast instead of mince here, as it is an inexpensive cut of meat that's perfect for slow cooking. Give it a try.

SERVES 4

750 g (1 lb 7 oz) breast of lamb, cut into 1 cm (½ inch) cubes

1 onion, sliced

1 carrot, cut into small dice

1 tablespoon chopped rosemary

1 heaped tablespoon tomato purée

500 ml (18 fl oz) lamb stock if using the conventional method or 200 ml (⅓ pint) boiling lamb stock if using the slow cooker method

2 tablespoons Worcestershire sauce

1 tablespoon mint sauce

800 g (1 lb 12 oz) Maris Piper potatoes, peeled and cubed (or use shop-bought mashed potatoes)

30 g (1 oz) unsalted butter

100 ml (3½ fl oz) milk, warmed

100 g (3½ oz) Cheddar cheese, grated

Broccoli or peas, to serve

CONVENTIONAL METHOD

1 Preheat the oven to 150°C (300°F), Gas Mark 2.
2 Season the lamb and sear in a very hot, dry, large, heavy-based casserole until golden. This is an important step because it will render away lots of the fat. Pour away most of the fat, then add the onion, carrot and rosemary and cook for 5 minutes, until softened.
3 Stir through the tomato purée for 30 seconds, then add the 500 ml (18 fl oz) of stock, the Worcestershire sauce and mint sauce. Give it all a good stir, then put on a tight-fitting lid and cook in the oven for 3 hours.
4 Meanwhile, make the mashed potatoes. Place the potatoes in a large saucepan and cover with water. Bring to a boil and simmer for about 15 minutes or until softened. Drain and then mash the potatoes along with the butter and warmed milk then season with salt and pepper. (Or if you're using my cheat of shop-bought mash, pop it in the microwave for 3 minutes and stir well.)
5 Remove the lamb from the casserole and use forks to shred the meat slightly, then return it to the casserole.
6 Increase the oven temperature to 180°C (350°F), Gas Mark 4.
7 Spread the mashed potatoes on top of the lamb mixture. Run the tines of a fork along the mash to give it some texture, then sprinkle on the cheese. Place back in the oven, uncovered, for 20 minutes. Leave to stand for 10 minutes before serving with broccoli or buttered peas on the side.

SLOW COOKER METHOD

1 Follow step 2 as above.
2 Add all the ingredients to your slow cooker apart from the mash and Cheddar, making sure you use only 200 ml (⅓ pint) of boiling stock. Cover and cook on the low setting for 7 hours.
3 Make the mashed potatoes as in step 4 above.
4 Remove the lamb from the slow cooker and use forks to shred the meat slightly. Spoon the lamb and the contents of the slow cooker into a large ovenproof baking dish, then follow steps 6–7 as above.

BRAISED FAGGOTS IN RICH CIDER GRAVY

People are put off by what they think goes into faggots, but they really are delicious, and when braised slowly in this rich cider gravy, they make a comforting and economical family meal. You can get incredible homemade faggots from your local butcher. I love to serve them with creamy, buttery mashed potatoes and seasonal greens.

SERVES 4

1–2 tablespoons olive oil

4 large or 8 small good-quality faggots

100 g (3½ oz) smoked pancetta or bacon lardons

1 large onion, thinly sliced

2 garlic cloves, crushed

1 tablespoon plain flour

300 ml (½ pint) medium-dry cider if using the conventional method or 200 ml (⅓ pint) if using the slow cooker method

300 ml (½ pint) chicken stock

1 tablespoon thyme leaves

1 teaspoon English mustard

To serve:
Mashed potatoes
Tenderstem broccoli

CONVENTIONAL METHOD

1 Preheat the oven to 190°C (375°F), Gas Mark 5.
2 Heat the oil in a large heavy-based casserole over a medium heat. Add the faggots and fry for 4–5 minutes, until they've formed a crust, then remove from the casserole and set aside. Pop in the pancetta, onion and garlic and cook for 2–3 minutes before adding the flour and cooking for a further minute.
3 Pour in the 300 ml (½ pint) of cider, stock, thyme and mustard and bring up to a simmer. Return the faggots to the casserole, cover with a tight-fitting lid and cook in the oven for 1 hour.
4 Serve with buttery mashed potatoes and Tenderstem broccoli with the rich cider gravy spooned over.

SLOW COOKER METHOD

1 Follow step 2 as above.
2 Pop the cooked pancetta, onion and garlic into the slow cooker. Pour in the 200 ml (⅓ pint) of cider, stock, thyme and mustard and stir well, then gently add the faggots. Cover and cook on the low setting for 7 hours. Turn the faggots once during the cooking time if you can.
3 Follow step 4 as above.

Try Something New

As a rule, when it comes to writing recipes my ethos is as follows: if I can't find an ingredient in my local supermarket or high street, then I don't include it in the recipe. I try to find an easier alternative.

But in this chapter I break my rule as there are some ingredients that are essential for a dish, whether it's a new ingredient like the gochujang red chilli paste in my Korean Beef Short Ribs or the achiote paste in my Cochinita Pibil Pork Tacos, or a cut of meat you might not be familiar with, like the flavour-packed ox cheeks for my Smoky Ox Cheek Chilli Nachos or the goat in my Caribbean Goat Curry.

Most of these ingredients can be found in the world-food aisle in your supermarket or have a hunt online, as there are some great suppliers out there that can get the ingredients to you in just a day or two.

Another suggestion is to start to build a good relationship with your local butcher. Some of these cuts are so-called throwaway cuts so the butcher might not have them in, but if you place an order a few days in advance, it won't be a problem. A lot of great food is in the planning. I get excited knowing I'm cooking for family and friends and try to plan what I'm cooking ahead of time. I also love to surprise people with ingredients and food that they might not normally try of their own accord.

RUSSIAN BRAISED BEEF AND STOUT CASSEROLE

This recipe was inspired by a recent trip to Russia to represent the UK in a charity football tournament. I'm a bad loser, so my runners-up medal didn't really cut it but it was an incredible experience and I got to try a whole new cuisine. The one dish I really did enjoy was a casserole of beautifully tender beef sweetened with prunes. When I got back to the UK I played around with this combination and found that pairing it with a bitter stout to braise the meat works wonderfully. Serve with a buttery mustard mash.

SERVES 4

1–2 tablespoons olive oil

700 g (1 lb 9 oz) beef skirt or chuck, cut into 2.5 cm (1 inch) pieces

2 tablespoons plain flour seasoned with salt and pepper

1 large onion, diced

2 celery sticks, finely diced

1 heaped tablespoon tomato purée

300 ml (½ pint) dark stout

500 ml (18 fl oz) beef stock if using the conventional method or 200 ml (⅓ pint) if using the slow cooker method

1 bay leaf

100 g (3½ oz) prunes, halved

Salt and pepper

Flat leaf parsley, to garnish

Mustard mashed potatoes, to serve

CONVENTIONAL METHOD

1 Preheat the oven to 160°C (325°F), Gas Mark 3.

2 Heat the oil in a large heavy-based casserole over a medium to high heat. Dust the beef in the seasoned flour, then add to the casserole and fry for 5–6 minutes, until golden. Do this in batches so you don't overcrowd the pan. Remove from the casserole and set aside. Add the onion and celery and cook for a few minutes, then add the tomato purée. Pour in the stout and scrape the bottom of the pan to make sure nothing is stuck.

3 Pour in the 500 ml (18 fl oz) of stock, then add the bay leaf and a pinch of salt and pepper and bring up to a simmer. Return the beef to the pan and cover with a tight-fitting lid. Cook in the oven for 3 hours.

4 Remove the casserole from the oven and add a splash of water if needed, then stir through the prunes and return to the oven for a further 2 hours.

5 Scatter over some flat leaf parsley to garnish before serving with a buttery mustard mash.

SLOW COOKER METHOD

1 Follow step 2 as above.

2 Pop the beef and onion mixture into your slow cooker, then pour in the 200 ml (⅓ pint) of stock and add the bay leaf and a pinch of salt and pepper. Put the lid on and cook on the low setting for 8 hours. Halfway through the cooking time, add the prunes. If you want a slightly thicker sauce, then pull the lid slightly ajar for the last hour.

3 Follow step 5 as above.

OLD BAY STEAM POT

A couple years ago I was lucky enough to have a holiday in Florida. One evening we visited a crab shack and I had my first experience of a steam pot of potatoes, corn on the cob, crab and shrimp. It was amazing. I asked what the secret was and it turned out to be a spice mix called Old Bay Seasoning, which is very easy to get online.

SERVES 4

500 ml (18 fl oz) lager if using the conventional method or 200 ml (⅓ pint) if using the slow cooker method

1 heaped tablespoon Old Bay Seasoning

600 g (1 lb 5 oz) new potatoes, halved

200 g (7 oz) uncured chorizo sausage, cut into bite-sized pieces

4 ears of sweetcorn, halved

500 g (1 lb 2 oz) large raw prawns

40 g (1½ oz) unsalted butter

2 garlic cloves, crushed

2 tablespoons chopped parsley

Juice of ½ lemon

5 spring onions, thinly sliced

Crusty bread, to serve

CONVENTIONAL METHOD

1 Preheat the oven to 180°C (350°F), Gas Mark 4.
2 Pour the 500 ml (18 fl oz) of lager into a large heavy-based casserole and add half of the Old Bay Seasoning. Bring to the boil, then add the potatoes, chorizo and sweetcorn. Give it a stir, then pop on a tight-fitting lid and transfer to the oven to cook for 1 hour.
3 Remove the casserole from the oven, add the prawns and stir well. Pop the lid back on and put back in the oven for 5 minutes, until the prawns have cooked through.
4 Meanwhile, melt the butter and stir through the garlic and parsley.
5 Remove the casserole from the oven and pour over the garlic butter and lemon juice, then sprinkle with the remaining Old Bay Seasoning and the spring onions. Bring to the table for everyone to dive in and serve with crusty bread to mop up those incredible juices.

SLOW COOKER METHOD

1 Pour the 200 ml (⅓ pint) of lager into your slow cooker and add half of the Old Bay Seasoning along with the potatoes, chorizo and sweetcorn. Cover and cook on the low setting for 7 hours.
2 Remove the lid and add the prawns, then pop the lid back on and cook on the high setting for a further 10 minutes.
3 Follow steps 4–5 as above.

TIP

If you can't find Old Bay Seasoning, try making your own. You can find a number of recipes online.

KOREAN BEEF
SHORT RIBS

Gochujang is a Korean red chilli paste that also contains fermented soya beans. Used in many dishes, this ingredient adds an incredible savoury flavour to these short ribs. I've actually broken one of my rules for this one – usually if I can't find an ingredient on my high street or in my local supermarket then I find alternatives, but this really is an ingredient you must get familiar with. It can be found in Asian markets or online, so just plan ahead a little.

SERVES 4

1–2 tablespoons olive oil

2 kg (4 lb 8 oz) meaty beef short ribs on the bone (approx. 4)

2 garlic cloves, crushed

1 thumb-sized piece of fresh root ginger, grated

100 ml (3½ fl oz) water

4 tablespoons soy sauce

4 tablespoons rice vinegar

3 tablespoons gochujang (Korean red chilli paste)

2 tablespoons soft dark brown sugar

To serve:

Spring onions, thinly sliced

1 tablespoon sesame seeds, toasted

Boiled rice

Kimchi

CONVENTIONAL METHOD

1 Preheat the oven to 150°C (300°F), Gas Mark 2.
2 Heat the oil in a large heavy-based casserole over a medium heat. Add the beef short ribs in batches and seal for 7–8 minutes, until golden, then set aside. Discard any fat in the casserole.
3 Add all the remaining ingredients to the casserole, stirring well, then return the ribs to the sauce. Cover with a tight-fitting lid and cook in the oven for 4 hours.
4 Before serving, sprinkle over the spring onions and sesame seeds. Serve with some fluffy boiled rice and kimchi.

SLOW COOKER METHOD

1 Follow step 2 as above.
2 Put all the remaining ingredients in your slow cooker, stirring well, then add the ribs to the sauce. Cover with the lid and cook on the low setting for 7 hours.
3 Follow step 4 as above.

COCHINITA PIBIL PORK TACOS

I was introduced to this dish by a friend of mine, Mark, who gave up a good job to chase his dream and start a taco street-food truck in a converted ice cream van. The first time I tried these, I fell in love with the shredded citrus pork topped generously with a punchy salsa, plus it's the perfect build-your-own family sharing dish. The annatto seeds or achiote paste can be purchased online, so plan ahead and order some in.

SERVES 4–6

1 kg (2 lb 4 oz) pork shoulder,
    cut into 2.5 cm (1 inch) pieces
1 onion, thinly sliced
Salt and pepper

Marinade:
6 whole cloves
2 tablespoons annatto seeds
    or 25 g (1 oz) achiote paste
1 tablespoon cumin seeds
½ teaspoon ground allspice
6 garlic cloves, crushed
1 green chilli, finely diced
Juice of 2 large oranges
Juice of 2 limes

Salsa:
150 g (5½ oz) roasted red peppers
    from a jar, finely chopped
100 g (3½ oz) baby plum tomatoes,
    finely chopped
1 dried chipotle chilli, rehydrated in
    boiling water and finely chopped
½ red onion, finely diced
2 tablespoons finely chopped fresh
    coriander
Juice of 1 lime
2 tablespoons olive oil

To serve:
Mini flour tortillas
1–2 ripe avocados, halved, pitted
    and sliced
Soured cream
Fresh coriander

CONVENTIONAL METHOD

1 Place the cubed pork in a large freezer bag or bowl. Grind the spices for the marinade in a pestle and mortar, then add the garlic and chilli and crush to a paste. Combine the spice paste with the orange and lime juice, then pour this over the meat, tossing to coat. Leave to marinate in the refrigerator for a couple of hours if you can.

2 Preheat the oven to 230°C (450°F), Gas Mark 8.

3 Place the onion in a roasting tin, then place the pork, including the marinade, on top and season with salt and pepper. Roast in the oven for 20 minutes. Lower the heat to 160°C (325°F), Gas Mark 3 and cover the joint tightly with foil, then return to the oven for 5 hours.

4 Remove from the oven and leave to rest for 30 minutes, then pull the pork apart using forks. Any resting juices can be mixed through the meat.

5 To make the salsa, put the roasted red peppers, tomatoes, chilli, onion and coriander into a bowl and season with salt and pepper, then dress with the lime juice and olive oil.

6 To serve, warm the tortillas and fill with the shredded pork. Top with salsa, avocado slices and a dollop of soured cream and garnish with a few fresh coriander leaves.

SLOW COOKER METHOD

1 Follow step 1 as above.

2 Place a bed of sliced onion in your slow cooker, then add the pork, including the marinade, and season with salt and pepper. Cover and cook on the low setting for 8 hours.

3 Remove the pork from the slow cooker and shred the meat with two forks. Follow steps 5–6 as above.

TIP

If you wish to thicken the sauce, mix 2 teaspoons of cornflour with a little water to form a smooth paste and stir into the pork mix after shredding.

SMOKY OX CHEEK CHILLI NACHOS

Nachos are one of my guilty pleasures, piled high and loaded to the brink of collapse. I've taken this comfort food classic to another level with the addition of the slow-cooked chilli beef. In this case I'm using a fantastic cut of beef, ox cheek. It's so underused but the flavour is incredible. Of course you can make your nachos whatever way you like, but I load mine up with salsa, cheese, jalapeños and a huge dollop of soured cream.

SERVES 4

1–2 tablespoons olive oil

2 ox cheeks, approx. 900 g (2 lb)

1 tablespoon plain flour seasoned with salt and pepper

1 large onion, diced

3 garlic cloves, crushed

1 heaped teaspoon smoked paprika

1 teaspoon ground cumin

1 teaspoon ground cinnamon

1 teaspoon dried oregano

½ teaspoon chilli powder

1 heaped tablespoon tomato purée

500 ml (18 fl oz) beef stock if using the conventional method or 200 ml (⅓ pint) if using the slow cooker method

1 teaspoon caster sugar (or to taste)

1 x 160 g (5¾ oz) bag of tortilla chips (you choose the flavour)

100 g (3½ oz) Mexicana Cheddar cheese, grated

CONVENTIONAL METHOD

1 Preheat the oven to 160°C (325°F), Gas Mark 3.

2 Heat the oil in a large heavy-based casserole over a medium to high heat. Dust the ox cheeks with the seasoned flour, then add to the casserole and brown for 3–4 minutes. Remove from the casserole and set aside.

3 Add the onion and garlic (or Time Saver Garlic Base) to the same pan and fry for 3–4 minutes. Add the smoked paprika, cumin, cinnamon, oregano and chilli powder and cook for another minute. Add the tomato purée and cook for a minute, then pour in the 500 ml (18 fl oz) of stock and bring to a simmer.

4 Return the ox cheeks to the casserole, then cover with a tight-fitting lid and transfer to the oven to cook for at least 4 hours.

5 Remove the casserole from the oven and increase the temperature to 200°C (400°F), Gas Mark 6. Remove the ox cheeks from the casserole and use forks to shred the meat, then return to the casserole. Season with salt and pepper and check for chilli heat, adding more chilli powder if necessary, then add the sugar to taste.

6 Scatter the tortilla chips onto an ovenproof plate, then spoon on the shredded beef and sprinkle over the cheese. Pop into the hot oven for 2–3 minutes, until the cheese has melted. Finish with some tomato salsa, pickled jalapeños and soured cream and scatter over some fresh coriander leaves.

TIME SAVER TIP
You could use 1 portion of the Time Saver Garlic Base on page 14 instead of the onion and garlic.

To serve:

Tomato salsa (*see* page 115)

Pickled jalapeños or 1 fresh red chilli,
    deseeded and thinly sliced

Soured cream

Fresh coriander

SLOW COOKER METHOD

1 Follow steps 2–3 as for the conventional method opposite, making sure you
  use only 200 ml (⅓ pint) of stock.
2 Carefully transfer the chilli braising liquid to your slow cooker, then add the
  ox cheeks and baste them. Cover with the lid and cook on the low setting for
  6 hours.
3 Preheat the oven to 200°C (400°F), Gas Mark 6.
4 Remove the ox cheeks from the slow cooker and use forks to shred the meat,
  then return the meat to the slow cooker. Season with salt and pepper and
  check for chilli heat, adding more chilli powder if necessary, then add the
  sugar to taste.
5 Follow step 6 as for the conventional method opposite.

OXTAIL BUNNY CHOW

Absolutely no bunnies were harmed in the testing of this recipe! Bunny chow is a classic South African dish of beef curry served in a hollowed-out loaf or crusty bread roll. It's street food at its finest. Once the curry has been demolished, you then eat the bread, which has soaked up all the fiery, spicy juices from the curry. If you don't fancy trying the oxtail, then replace it with another 400 g (14 oz) of cubed skirt steak.

SERVES 4

1–2 tablespoons olive oil

700 g (1 lb 9 oz) oxtail

400 g (14 oz) skirt steak, cut into
2.5 cm (1 inch) cubes

2 tablespoons plain flour seasoned
with salt and pepper

2 onions, sliced

3 garlic cloves, crushed

1 thumb-sized piece of fresh root
ginger, grated

1 green chilli, deseeded and diced

6 whole cloves

4 cardamom pods, lightly crushed

1 cinnamon stick or ½ teaspoon
ground cinnamon

1 star anise

1 heaped tablespoon garam masala

1 teaspoon nigella seeds

1 teaspoon mustard seeds

1 teaspoon ground turmeric

2 tablespoons tomato purée

CONVENTIONAL METHOD

1 Heat the oil in a large heavy-based casserole over a medium to high heat. Dust the meat with the flour, then add to the casserole in batches and seal for 5–6 minutes, until golden. Remove from the casserole and set aside.

2 Add the onions, garlic, ginger (or Time Saver Curry Base) and chilli and fry for 5 minutes before adding the spices and cooking for a couple more minutes. Add the tomato purée and cook for a further minute. Pour in the 800 ml (28 fl oz) of stock and coconut milk and bring up to a simmer.

3 Return the meat to the casserole and add the potatoes. Put the lid on and cook over a gentle heat for 3 hours.

4 Remove the oxtail from the casserole and shred the meat from the bone. Return to the casserole and cook, uncovered, for another 15–20 minutes, until the sauce has reduced and thickened.

5 Towards the end of the cooking time, make the sambal. Mix the carrots with the onion, sprinkle over the salt and leave for 10 minutes, then drain the excess liquid. Add the rest of the ingredients and allow to stand for 20 minutes.

6 Spoon into the hollowed-out rolls and garnish with the finely chopped fresh coriander. Serve the carrot and onion sambal on the side.

TIME SAVER TIP
You could use 2 portions of the Time Saver Curry Base on page 14 instead of the onion, garlic and ginger.

RECIPE CONTINUES ON PAGE 122

800 ml (28 fl oz) beef stock if using
 the conventional method or
 400 ml (14 fl oz) if using the
 slow cooker method
1 x 400 ml (14 fl oz) can of coconut milk
400 g (14 oz) Maris Piper potatoes, cut
 into small cubes
2 small bakers' loaves or 4 rolls, halved
 and hollowed out
Finely chopped fresh coriander, to
 garnish

Carrot and onion sambal
2 carrots, julienned or grated
1 red onion, thinly sliced
1 teaspoon salt
1 garlic clove, crushed
1 green chilli, deseeded and finely
 chopped
Juice of 1 lemon
1 teaspoon caster sugar

SLOW COOKER METHOD

1 Follow steps 1–2 as for the conventional method on page 120, making sure you use only 400 ml (14 fl oz) of stock.
2 Put the meat and potatoes in the slow cooker, then carefully pour in the stock mixture. Cover with the lid and cook on the low setting for 8 hours.
3 Follow step 5 as on page 120.
4 Remove the oxtail from the slow cooker and shred the meat from the bone, then stir the meat back into the slow cooker.
5 Follow step 6 as on page 120.

TIP

Leave the bread from the hollowed-out rolls to go stale, then grate it and freeze for handy breadcrumbs.

CARIBBEAN GOAT CURRY

A staple of Caribbean cuisine for many years, goat is starting to hit the mainstream in the UK, appearing on restaurant menus up and down the country, and it's perfect for slow cooking. I like to order my Jamaican curry powder online for an authentic taste of the Caribbean, but a mild or medium supermarket version will do the job too. Scotch bonnet chillies are fiery, so I pop mine but leave it whole and let the heat leach out into the curry. If you like more heat, though, feel free to chop it up into the sauce, just don't say I didn't warn you! I love this with classic rice and peas and festivals, which are deep-fried cornmeal dumplings.

SERVES 4

1–2 tablespoons olive oil

800 g (1 lb 12 oz) goat meat, cut into chunks

3 spring onions, sliced

1 onion, finely diced

3 garlic cloves, crushed

5–6 thyme sprigs

4 tablespoons mild curry powder

1 heaped tablespoon tomato purée

600 ml (20 fl oz) chicken stock if using the conventional method or 400 ml (14 fl oz) if using the slow cooker method

600 g (1 lb 5 oz) Maris Piper potatoes, cut into bite-sized pieces

1 Scotch bonnet chilli

Salt and pepper

To serve:

Boiled rice

Peas

Festival dumplings

CONVENTIONAL METHOD

1 Heat the oil in a large heavy-based casserole over a medium heat. Season the goat with salt and pepper, then add to the casserole and brown for 5–6 minutes, until golden. Add the spring onions, diced onion, garlic and thyme and cook for 5 minutes. Stir through the curry powder and tomato purée and cook for 2 minutes.

2 Pour in the 600 ml (20 fl oz) of stock and stir well before adding the potatoes. Pop the Scotch bonnet chilli with your fingers and add to the pot. This will add heat but won't overpower the dish.

3 Bring to a simmer, then cover and cook on a low heat for at least 2 hours. To thicken the sauce, remove the lid and reduce until it's the consistency you want.

4 Serve with boiled rice and peas, and if you're really pushing the boat out, with the deep-fried Jamaican cornmeal dumplings called festivals.

SLOW COOKER METHOD

1 Follow step 1 as above.

2 Transfer the meat mixture to your slow cooker, then pour in the 400 ml (14 fl oz) of stock and add the potatoes. Pop the Scotch bonnet chilli with your fingers and add to the slow cooker. This will add heat but won't overpower the dish. Stir well, then put on the lid and cook on the low setting for 8 hours.

3 Follow step 4 as above.

TIP

Wash your hands well after handling the Scotch bonnet chilli and avoid touching your eyes (or any other sensitive areas) for a while afterwards.

PORK AND BEAN CASSOULET

I was chatting to my local butcher about inexpensive cuts of meat that are perfect for slow cooking, and the one cut he couldn't believe isn't used more is the humble pig cheek. Because they have a natural marbling, during the slow cooking process they become so, so tender. Paired with this cider sauce and some creamy mashed potatoes, it's really worth asking your butcher to source some for you.

SERVES 4

1–2 tablespoons olive oil

400 g (14 oz) pig cheeks

1 heaped tablespoon plain flour seasoned with salt and pepper

1 onion, sliced

3 garlic cloves, crushed

3–4 thyme sprigs

1 bay leaf

½ teaspoon smoked paprika

300 ml (½ pint) dry cider

1 x 400 g (14 oz) can of cannellini beans, drained and rinsed

300 ml (½ pint) chicken stock

1 heaped tablespoon crème fraîche

Salt and pepper

Mashed potatoes, to serve

CONVENTIONAL METHOD

1 Heat the oil in a large heavy-based casserole over a medium to high heat. Dust the pig cheeks in the seasoned flour, then add to the casserole and fry for 5–6 minutes, until coloured. Remove from the casserole and set aside.

2 Pop the onion and garlic (or Time Saver Garlic Base) into the casserole and cook for a few minutes. Add the thyme, bay leaf and smoked paprika, then pour in the cider and let it reduce a little, scraping up any bits from the bottom of the pan. Add the beans and stock, then add the cheeks back in.

3 Cover with a lid and simmer for 3 hours over a gentle heat. Before serving, stir in the crème fraîche and check the seasoning.

4 While the pork is cooking, make the citrus crumb. Heat the oil in a pan over a medium heat, then throw in the breadcrumbs and garlic and cook for 2–3 minutes, until golden. Stir through the lemon zest and parsley.

5 Serve the cassoulet in wide bowls with some buttery mash and a sprinkling of the citrus crumb.

TIME SAVER TIP
You could use 1 portion of the Time Saver Garlic Base on page 14 instead of the onion and garlic.

Citrus crumb:
2 tablespoons olive oil
100 g (3½ oz) ciabatta bread, grated
2 garlic cloves, crushed
Zest of 1 unwaxed lemon
2 tablespoons chopped flat leaf
    parsley

SLOW COOKER METHOD

1 Follow step 1 as for the conventional method opposite.
2 Place all the cassoulet ingredients except the crème fraîche into your slow cooker and mix well, then gently add the golden pig cheeks. Cover and cook on the low setting for 6 hours. Before serving, stir in the crème fraîche and check the seasoning.
3 Follow steps 4–5 as for the conventional method opposite.

BEEF SHIN OSSO BUCCO

This traditional Italian dish is absolute comfort food for me. Veal shin is the cut that is usually cooked slowly in this rich sauce, but since veal isn't readily available I decided to give it a go with its beef counterpart, and it's delicious. Creamy mashed potatoes or a 50/50 parsnip and potato mash is the perfect accompaniment for this recipe.

SERVES 4

1–2 tablespoons olive oil
2 pieces of beef shin, approx.
    400–500 g (14 oz–1 lb 2 oz) each,
    2.5 cm (1 inch) thick, bone in
30 g (1 oz) plain flour seasoned with
    salt and pepper
1 large onion, finely diced
1 large carrot, finely diced
2 celery sticks, finely diced
1 heaped tablespoon tomato purée
100 ml (3½ fl oz) white wine
1 x 400 g (14 oz) can of chopped
    tomatoes
1 bay leaf
400 ml (14 fl oz) beef stock
Salt and pepper
Mashed potatoes, to serve

Gremolata:
Zest of 1 unwaxed lemon
2 garlic cloves, crushed
2 tablespoons chopped flat leaf
    parsley

CONVENTIONAL METHOD

1 Heat the oil in a large heavy-based casserole over a high heat. Dust the beef shin with the seasoned flour, then add to the casserole and fry for 6–7 minutes, until browned. Remove from the casserole and set aside. Add the finely diced onion, carrot and celery and sweat down for 5 minutes, until softened, then stir in the tomato purée and cook for a further minute.

2 Pour in the white wine and deglaze the pan, then add the chopped tomatoes and bay leaf, pop the beef back in and add enough stock to just cover the beef.

3 Pop on a lid and cook over a low heat for around 2 hours. If you would like a thicker sauce, raise the heat and remove the lid for the last 20 minutes. Season with salt and pepper.

4 To make the gremolata, mix together the lemon zest, garlic and parsley. Just before serving, stir it through the osso bucco. I like to reserve some for garnish. Serve with creamy mashed potatoes.

SLOW COOKER METHOD

1 Follow step 1 as above. You can skip this step, but it will add lots of flavour. Pour in the wine and reduce by half, scraping up any bits from the pan.

2 Pour the chopped tomatoes and stock into your slow cooker and stir well. Stir through the vegetables and the sauce, then add the seared beef shin. Pop in the bay leaf and a sprinkling of seasoning. Put on the lid and cook on the low setting for 7 hours.

3 Follow step 4 as above.

TIP

You can use diced beef shin (you need approx. 200–250 g, 7–9 oz, per person), but ask your butcher for a couple of pieces of marrowbone to throw in the pot.

BEEF BRISKET FRENCH DIP ROLLS

I'm always looking for time-saving cheats in the kitchen and ways to make my life simpler. Using a can of beef consommé saves all the hard work of preparing this flavour-packed beef stock. This recipe can literally be in the oven or slow cooker, working its slow-cooked magic, within 10 minutes. I became obsessed with these French dip rolls after seeing them being eaten on TV shows like Man v. Food. They always look so good that I had to try them for myself.

SERVES 4

1–2 tablespoons olive oil
600 g (1 lb 5 oz) beef brisket joint
2 onions, sliced
1 garlic clove, crushed
1 x 400 g (14 oz) can of beef
  consommé
2 tablespoons Worcestershire sauce
2 thyme sprigs, leaves picked
1 bay leaf
Salt and pepper

To serve:
4 brioche rolls, halved
Dijon mustard
4 slices of Swiss cheese

CONVENTIONAL METHOD

1 Preheat the oven to 160°C (325°F), Gas Mark 3.
2 Heat the oil in a large heavy-based casserole over a high heat. Season the brisket with salt and pepper, then add to the casserole and sear for 6–7 minutes, until golden. Remove from the casserole and set aside. Reduce the heat, then add the onions and garlic (or Time Saver Garlic Base) and gently cook for 5 minutes, until golden and soft.
3 Pour in the consommé and Worcestershire sauce, then pop the brisket back into the casserole along with the thyme and bay leaf. Bring up to a gentle simmer, then cover with a tight-fitting lid and pop into the oven to cook for 3 hours.
4 Remove the brisket from the pan and allow to rest for 10 minutes before slicing thinly against the grain of the meat. Strain the onions from the liquid, then return the gravy to the casserole to keep warm.
5 Preheat the grill.
6 Spread the base of each roll with mustard, then add plenty of the sliced beef, the reserved onions and finally a slice of Swiss cheese. Pop under the hot grill just until the cheese melts, then place the top of the bun on. Serve the rolls with a small bowl of the gravy on the side for dipping.

SLOW COOKER METHOD

1 Follow step 2 as above.
2 Transfer the brisket, onions, consommé, Worcestershire sauce and herbs to your slow cooker. Put the lid on and cook on the low setting for 8 hours.
3 Remove the brisket and allow to rest for 10 minutes before slicing thinly against the grain of the meat. Strain the onions from the liquid, then return the gravy to the slow cooker to keep warm.
4 Follow steps 5–6 as above.

TIME SAVER TIP
You could use 2 portions of the Time Saver Garlic Base on page 14 instead of the onions and garlic.

WHOLE ROASTED CAULIFLOWER WITH TOMATOES AND OLIVES

If there is one vegetable that's seriously underrated, it's the humble cauliflower. Now when it's boiled to death, like the way I used to eat it as a kid, it's pointless. Smothered in a cheese sauce, even though totally amazing, is just a vehicle for the cheese. But then I discovered roasted cauliflower and it was a game changer. Cauliflower steaks are great, but for pure theatrics, this whole-roasted brassica is a winner.

SERVES 4

1–2 tablespoons olive oil

1 onion, very finely diced

3 garlic cloves, crushed

1 x 400 g (14 oz) can of chopped tomatoes

400 ml (14 fl oz) vegetable stock if using the conventional method or 200 ml (⅓ pint) if using the slow cooker method

1 teaspoon dried oregano

½ teaspoon chilli powder (optional)

1 whole cauliflower

50 g (1¾ oz) butter, melted

100 g (3½ oz) pitted green and black olives

2 tablespoons chopped parsley

Salt and pepper

Parmesan cheese, to serve

CONVENTIONAL METHOD

1 Preheat the oven to 180°C (350°F), Gas Mark 4.

2 Heat the oil in a large heavy-based casserole over a medium heat. Add the onion and garlic (or Time Saver Garlic Base) and cook for 5 minutes, until softened. Add the tomatoes, 400 ml (14 fl oz) of stock, the oregano, chilli powder and a pinch of salt and pepper. Brush the cauliflower with the melted butter, then season that with salt and pepper too. Pop into the casserole, cut side down, cover with a tight-fitting lid and cook in the oven for 1 hour. Remove from the oven and baste with more butter. Add a little water if the sauce is too thick then return to the oven and cook, uncovered, for another 20 minutes, until the cauliflower is golden.

3 Stir through the olives and parsley, then grate over some Parmesan. Bring to the table and serve a large wedge with some of the lovely tomato sauce.

SLOW COOKER METHOD

1 If you have time, fry the onion and garlic as in step 2 above (or just use the Time Saver Garlic Base), then pop this into your slow cooker along with the tomatoes, 200 ml (⅓ pint) of stock, oregano, chilli powder and a pinch of salt and pepper. Brush the cauliflower with the melted butter, then season that with salt and pepper too. Pop into the slow cooker, cover and cook on the low setting for 6 hours.

2 Remove the cauliflower from the slow cooker, then stir the olives and parsley through the sauce. Spoon the sauce onto a serving plate, then top with the cauliflower before grating over some Parmesan.

TIME SAVER TIP
You could use 1 portion of the Time Saver Garlic Base on page 14 instead of the onion and garlic.

ROHIM'S IFTAR MUTTON CURRY

Last year I was lucky enough to be invited to celebrate Iftar with my friends the Uddin family. I got to spend the day in the kitchen with my pal Rohim, who taught me this incredible mutton curry, which was happily enjoyed by all. Mutton isn't as widely available as lamb, but there's no comparison in flavour, so do try to seek it out or ask your local butcher to get some in for you. If you can get hold of some lamb bones you can throw these in the pot too as they will add loads of flavour.

SERVES 4

1–2 tablespoons olive oil
600 g (1 lb 12 oz) boneless shoulder of
    mutton, cut into 2.5 cm (1 inch) cubes
2 tablespoons butter or ghee
2 onions, thinly sliced
5 garlic cloves, crushed
1 green chilli, diced
1 thumb-sized piece of fresh root
    ginger, grated
1 cinnamon stick
1 bay leaf
2 tablespoons garam masala
1 teaspoon paprika
½ teaspoon ground turmeric
500 ml (18 fl oz) lamb stock if using
    the conventional method or
    300 ml (½ pint) if using the
    slow cooker method
1 x 400 g (14 oz) can of chopped
    tomatoes
Pinch of salt

To serve:
Basmati rice
Naan bread

TIME SAVER TIP
You could use 2 portions of the Time
Saver Curry Base on page 14 instead
of the onions, garlic and ginger.

CONVENTIONAL METHOD

1 Heat the oil in a large heavy-based casserole over a medium to high heat. Add the mutton pieces and fry for 3–4 minutes, until golden. Remove from the casserole and set aside. Add the butter and onions and cook over a low heat for 10 minutes, stirring frequently. Add the garlic, chilli, ginger (or Time Saver Curry Base) and spices and cook for 2 minutes.

2 Pour in the 500 ml (18 fl oz) of stock and the chopped tomatoes. Return the meat to the casserole and add a good pinch of salt, then cover and cook over a low heat for 3 hours.

3 Serve with basmati rice and naan bread.

SLOW COOKER METHOD

1 Follow step 1 as for the conventional method opposite.

2 Add all the ingredients to your slow cooker, making sure you use only 300 ml (½ pint) of stock. Cover and cook on the low setting for 8 hours.

3 Follow step 3 as for the conventional method opposite.

CHICKEN KORMA BUT NOT AS YOU KNOW IT

I'm guessing you might have tried a korma at one point in your life – creamy, sweet, full of almonds, coconut and raisins? Well, this version from my mate Rohim is nothing like that. Even though it is rich with butter and ghee, it relies on slow-cooking the onions to extract the maximum sweetness. Chillies are optional, but if you split them in half and remove before serving, they add a lovely background heat to my take on this classic curry house favourite.

SERVES 4

800 g (1 lb 12 oz) skinless chicken thighs, bone in
150 ml (¼ pint) natural yogurt
1 teaspoon garam masala
1½ teaspoons ground turmeric
1–2 tablespoons olive oil
6 onions, thinly sliced
40 g (1½ oz) butter or ghee
3 tablespoons olive oil
5 garlic cloves, crushed
1 thumb-sized piece of fresh root ginger, grated
3 bird's-eye chillies, halved (feel free to add as many as you like!)
2 cardamom pods, lightly crushed
2 bay leaves
1 cinnamon stick
1 heaped tablespoon garam masala
½ teaspoon chilli powder
500 ml (18 fl oz) chicken stock if using the conventional method or 250 ml (9 fl oz) if using the slow cooker method
Salt and pepper

TIME SAVER TIP
You could use 3 portions of the Time Saver Curry Base on page 14 instead of the onions, garlic and ginger.

CONVENTIONAL METHOD

1 Place the chicken pieces into a large freezer bag, then add the yogurt, garam masala and half a teaspoon of ground turmeric. Massage to make sure all the chicken is well coated, then seal the bag and leave to marinate overnight.
2 The next day, preheat the oven to 160°C (325°F), Gas Mark 3.
3 Heat the oil in a large heavy-based casserole over a medium heat. Shake any excess marinade from the chicken, add the chicken to the casserole and sear until golden, which will take 4–5 minutes. Remove from the casserole and set aside.
4 Add the sliced onions along with the butter or ghee and the oil. Cook on a very low heat for 20–30 minutes, stirring frequently. The onions should be golden and sticky. Add the garlic and ginger and cook for a further 2–3 minutes. (Or you could use the Time Saver Curry Base.) Add the bird's-eye chillies, cardamom, bay leaves, cinnamon stick and ground spices, including the remaining teaspoon of turmeric.
5 Pour in the 500 ml (18 fl oz) of stock, then bring up to a gentle simmer and season with salt and pepper. Place the chicken pieces back into the casserole, then cover with a tight-fitting lid and cook in the oven for 2 hours. Halfway through cooking, give it a stir and add a little more stock if needed.

SLOW COOKER METHOD

1 Follow steps 1, 3 and 4 as above.
2 Transfer the onions to your slow cooker, then add the 250 ml (9 fl oz) of stock and some salt and pepper. Stir well. Place the chicken on top of the onion base, then pop the lid on. Cook on the low setting for 7 hours.

VENISON MEATBALLS IN RED WINE

I love the mild game flavour of venison. The shoulder and leg are ideal cuts for slow cooking, but my eyes lit up when I saw venison sausages in my local supermarket, so I thought I'd do something a little different with them.

SERVES 4

6 venison sausages, approx. 300 g (10½ oz)
2 garlic cloves, crushed
40 g (1½ oz) breadcrumbs
2 tablespoons plain flour seasoned with salt and pepper
1–2 tablespoons olive oil
2 onions, finely diced
1 large carrot, finely diced
3 celery sticks, finely diced
100 g (3½ oz) smoked pancetta or smoked streaky bacon, cubed
1 bay leaf
1 tablespoon finely chopped rosemary
1 tablespoon juniper berries, crushed in a pestle and mortar
2 heaped tablespoons tomato purée
500 ml (18 fl oz) red wine if using the conventional method or 200 ml (⅓ pint) if using the slow cooker method
500 ml (18 fl oz) beef stock if using the conventional method or 300 ml (½ pint) if using the slow cooker method
30 g (1 oz) dark chocolate, at least 70 per cent cocoa solids, grated
1 heaped tablespoon redcurrant jelly
Salt and pepper

To serve:
Mashed potatoes
Parmesan cheese
Snipped chives

CONVENTIONAL METHOD

1   Squeeze the sausages out of their casings into a large bowl. Add the garlic and breadcrumbs and mix to combine. Roll into 12 equal-sized meatballs and dust in the seasoned flour.
2   Heat the oil in a large heavy-based casserole over a medium heat. Add the meatballs and fry for 4–5 minutes, until they have formed a crust. Remove from the casserole and set aside.
3   Add the onions, carrot, celery, pancetta, herbs and juniper berries and cook over a low to medium heat for a further 6–7 minutes before adding the tomato purée and cooking for a further couple of minutes. Pour in the 500 ml (18 fl oz) of red wine and reduce by half.
4   Add the meatballs back in along with the 500 ml (18 fl oz) of stock and stir to combine. Bring up to a gentle simmer, then cover and cook over a low heat for 2 hours, stirring occasionally.
5   Season with salt and pepper to taste, then add the chocolate and redcurrant jelly and stir until well combined.
6   Serve with some buttery mashed potatoes, a grating of Parmesan and some snipped chives.

SLOW COOKER METHOD

1   Follow steps 1–3 as above, making sure you use only 200 ml (⅓ pint) of red wine.
2   Transfer the ingredients to your slow cooker along with the meatballs and 300 ml (½ pint) of stock. Put on the lid and cook on the low setting for 5 hours.
3   Follow steps 5 and 6 as above.

Store Cupboard Suppers

For those times when even the best intentions to plan your weekly meals have gone out the window, this chapter might be right up your street. These recipes are all about ease. I know I talk about enjoying the process that comes with putting a meal on the table, but sometimes circumstances don't allow that.

There are a few cheats here, like the can of beef consommé in the deeply rich French Onion Soup and the quick and easy filo pastry topping on the Chicken and Mushroom Mini Pot Pies. There are certain ingredients that I like to keep the cupboards stocked with. Soups, chickpeas and couscous are all dead handy for knocking up a great meal without having to make a special trip to the shops.

There are some proper comfort food recipes in this chapter too – it's not all about chucking everything from the cupboards into one recipe. Sometimes it's about thinking outside the box, being creative and using tinned goods like soups to make sauces or chickpeas to bulk out recipes to make delicious and inexpensive dinners like my Moroccan Chickpea Stew.

It's time to use those jars, cans and dried goods in your cupboards and refrigerator and get cooking these amazing store cupboard suppers.

MOROCCAN MINCED LAMB STEW WITH PAPRIKA DUMPLINGS

There's a trick to cooking mince in the slow cooker: you always need to get it crisp and golden in a hot pan first, otherwise all the unnecessary fats will become part of the dish. Dumplings were a childhood favourite of mine, adding texture while at the same time absorbing the delicious flavours of the stew they are cooked in. Experiment by adding herbs to yours to take them to another level. I love to eat this stew with some crispy sauté potatoes.

SERVES 4

2 tablespoons olive oil
500 g (1 lb 2 oz) minced lamb
2 onions, diced
1 large carrot, diced
4 garlic cloves, crushed
2 teaspoons harissa paste
1 teaspoon smoked paprika
1 teaspoon ground cinnamon
1 teaspoon ground cumin
3 roasted red peppers from a jar,
    finely chopped
60 g (2¼ oz) dried apricots, chopped
600 ml (20 fl oz) lamb stock if using
    the conventional method or
    350 ml (12 fl oz) boiling lamb stock
    if using the slow cooker method
250 ml (9 fl oz) tomato passata
2 tablespoons tomato purée
1 tablespoon honey
Salt and pepper

Paprika dumplings:
120 g (4¼ oz) self-raising flour
60 g (2¼ oz) beef suet
1 tablespoon chopped fresh
    coriander
1 heaped teaspoon smoked paprika
Good pinch of salt
70 ml (2½ fl oz) cold water

To serve:
Fresh coriander, to garnish
Sauté potatoes

CONVENTIONAL METHOD

1 Preheat the oven to 160°C (325°F), Gas Mark 3.
2 Heat 1 tablespoon of oil in a large heavy-based casserole over a high heat. Add the minced lamb and brown until crisp and golden, then transfer to a bowl with a slotted spoon and set aside. Drain off the excess fat left behind in the casserole, then add another tablespoon of oil. Add the onions, carrot and garlic and cook until softened, which will take around 5 minutes.
3 Stir through the harissa and spices and cook for a further minute. Add the roasted red peppers, apricots, 600 ml (20 fl oz) of stock, passata, tomato purée and honey and season with salt and pepper. Return the mince to the pan and bring up to a simmer, then cover with a tight-fitting lid and cook in the oven for 2 hours.
4 Meanwhile, make the dumplings by mixing together the flour, suet, coriander, paprika and salt. Add the water a little at a time – you need enough water to bind the dumplings but you don't want the dough to be too wet. Make into eight dumplings.
5 Remove the casserole from the oven and raise the temperature to 180°C (350°F), Gas Mark 4. Place the dumplings on top of the stew and put back in the oven, uncovered, for a further 30 minutes.
6 Garnish with fresh coriander and serve with sauté potatoes.

SLOW COOKER METHOD

1 Follow step 2 as above.
2 Add the minced lamb, the onion mixture and all the other ingredients to your slow cooker, making sure you use only 350 ml (12 fl oz) of boiling stock, and stir well. Put the lid on and cook on the high setting for 2 hours or the low setting for 4 hours. Season with salt and pepper.
3 Make the dumplings as in step 4 above. Place in the slow cooker, then turn the setting to high and cook for a further hour.
4 Follow step 6 as above.

MUSHROOM AND LENTIL COTTAGE PIE

I love lentils, especially the nuttiness of Puy lentils, and the ready-to-eat packs are a great store cupboard standby. My mushroom and lentil cottage pie is a delicious meat-free option for any night of the week.

SERVES 4

1–2 tablespoons olive oil
300 g (10½ oz) chestnut mushrooms, trimmed and quartered
1 onion, diced
1 large carrot, finely diced
3 celery sticks, finely diced
4 thyme sprigs, leaves picked
1 heaped tablespoon tomato purée
100 ml (3½ fl oz) red wine (optional)
300 ml (½ pint) boiling water
1 heaped tablespoon gravy granules
250 g (9 oz) ready-to-eat Puy lentils
Salt and pepper

Sweet potato topping:
800 g (1 lb 12 oz) sweet potatoes, diced
20 g (¾ oz) unsalted butter
80 ml (2¾ fl oz) warm milk
1 heaped tablespoon wholegrain mustard
80 g (2¾ oz) Cheddar cheese, grated

CONVENTIONAL METHOD

1 Heat a splash of oil in a large pan over a high heat. Add the mushrooms and brown for 5–6 minutes, until golden. Remove from the pan and set aside. Add another splash of oil, then the diced veg and fry for around 5 minutes. Return the mushrooms to the pan along with the thyme, tomato purée and red wine (if using). Reduce the red wine by half.

2 Mix the boiling water and gravy granules together and stir until fully combined. Pour into the pan along with the lentils, then simmer over a low heat, uncovered, for 20–30 minutes until reduced down and thickened slightly. Season with salt and pepper. Add a little more water if it's thickening too much.

3 While the lentils are simmering, preheat the oven to 200°C (400°F), Gas Mark 6.

4 Boil the sweet potatoes until softened, then drain and mash with the butter, warm milk and mustard until smooth. Season with salt and pepper.

5 Transfer the lentils to a large baking dish and top with the sweet potato mash. Run the tines of a fork over the top of the potatoes to give them some texture, then sprinkle over the grated cheese. Bake in the oven for 30 minutes, until golden.

SLOW COOKER METHOD

1 Follow step 1 as above.

2 Mix the boiling water and gravy granules together and stir until fully combined. Add to your slow cooker along with the lentils and the contents of the pan. Cover and cook on the low setting for 6 hours. Season with salt and pepper.

3 Follow step 4 as above, then spoon the mash over the lentils. Run the tines of a fork over the top of the potatoes to give them some texture, then sprinkle over the grated cheese. Turn the setting up to high and cook for a further 30 minutes. Alternatively, you could finish the pie in the oven preheated to 200°C (400°F), Gas Mark 6 if you want a crispy potato topping.

JERKED CHICKEN

I grew up eating jerked chicken cooked over coals in huge steel drums. My take on this classic is totally not authentic, so I don't want my friends from the Caribbean to give me a hard time! This is probably one of the simplest recipes in the book and is proof that delicious food doesn't require a long list of ingredients and complicated cooking. The fiery jerk spices are cooled down by enjoying this dish with a side of creamy coleslaw and some rice and beans or coconut rice.

SERVES 4

4 large chicken thighs, bone in and skin on
1 tablespoon olive oil (slow cooker method only)

Marinade:
30 g (1 oz) jerk paste (I like the Dunns River brand)
2 tablespoons sweet chilli sauce
2 tablespoons soy sauce
1 tablespoon thyme leaves
1 tablespoon tomato purée
1 tablespoon red wine vinegar

To serve:
Coleslaw
Rice and beans or coconut rice
Lime wedges

CONVENTIONAL METHOD

1 Trim away any excess skin from the chicken thighs, then slash the top of each thigh three times. Place all the marinade ingredients in a large bowl and mix well, then add the chicken and make sure it's well coated with the sauce. If time allows, cover and leave in the refrigerator for at least 2 hours to allow the flavours to develop.
2 Preheat the oven to 190°C (375°F), Gas Mark 5.
3 Place the chicken on a baking tray, skin side up, and cook in the oven for 50–60 minutes, until cooked through.
4 Serve with a side of creamy coleslaw and some rice and beans or coconut rice with lime wedges on the side.

SLOW COOKER METHOD

1 Trim away any excess skin from the chicken thighs, then slash the top of each thigh three times. Heat the oil in a pan over a medium to high heat, then add the chicken, skin side down, and fry until golden, which will take around 5 minutes.
2 Put all the marinade ingredients in your slow cooker and stir until fully combined. Add the thighs to the slow cooker one at a time and coat in the sauce, turning so they are all skin side up. Cover with the lid and cook on the low setting for 6 hours.
3 Pull the lid slightly to one side, leaving a 2.5 cm (1 inch) gap, and cook for a further hour, until the chicken is cooked through.
4 Follow step 4 as above.

SMOKY CHORIZO POTATO HASH WITH LAGER CHEESE SAUCE

Who would have thought that you could cook these crisp and golden new potatoes spiked with the smokiness of chorizo sausage in a slow cooker? These are a real treat for me and I love to load them up, doused with the cheese sauce, drizzled with soured cream and topped with some fiery jalapeños.

SERVES 4

1 kg (2 lb 4 oz) new potatoes, cut into bite-sized pieces

200 g (7 oz) uncured chorizo sausage, cut into bite-sized pieces

1 onion, diced

1 tablespoon olive oil

1 teaspoon ground cumin

½ teaspoon smoked paprika

Salt and pepper

Lager cheese sauce:

25 g (1 oz) unsalted butter

2 garlic cloves, crushed

25 g (1 oz) plain flour

1 x 330 ml (11½ fl oz) can of Mexican lager (I like Corona)

70 ml (2½ fl oz) milk

150 g (5½ oz) Mexicana Cheddar cheese, grated, plus extra to serve

To serve:

Soured cream

Fresh jalapeños, sliced (optional)

Fresh coriander

CONVENTIONAL METHOD

1 Preheat the oven to 180°C (350°F), Gas Mark 4.

2 Place the potatoes, chorizo, onion, olive oil and spices in a large bowl along with a pinch of salt and pepper and mix well. Scatter onto a baking tray and cook in the oven for 45–50 minutes until the potatoes are golden and the chorizo is cooked through.

3 Meanwhile, to make the lager cheese sauce, melt the butter over a low to medium heat along with the garlic, then whisk in the flour and cook for 2–3 minutes. Gradually pour in the lager and milk, whisking as you go, and continue whisking until thickened and smooth. Stir in the cheese and season with salt and pepper.

4 Divide the potatoes and chorizo between 4 plates. Drizzle over the cheese sauce and soured cream, then scatter over extra Mexicana cheese, the jalapeños (if using) and a few fresh coriander leaves.

SLOW COOKER METHOD

1 Place the potatoes, chorizo, onion, olive oil and spices in a large bowl along with a pinch of salt and pepper and mix well. Scatter into your slow cooker, then put on the lid and cook on the high setting for 3 hours, stirring occasionally.

2 Follow steps 3–4 as above.

FRENCH ONION SOUP WITH BLUE CHEESE CROUTONS

When I was testing recipes for this book I was surprised by just how versatile a slow cooker actually is. The fact that you can slow cook your onions until they are beautiful, sweet and tender without having to watch them like a hawk was a revelation. What I like to do with this recipe is pop the onions on overnight and give them a good stir in the morning, then add the rest of the ingredients a couple of hours before dinnertime.

SERVES 4

3 tablespoons olive oil
40 g (1½ oz) unsalted butter
3 large onions, thinly sliced
2 garlic cloves, crushed
3–4 thyme sprigs
2 bay leaves
1 teaspoon caster sugar
2 tablespoons sherry vinegar
2 x 400 g (14 oz) cans of beef
    consommé
200 ml (⅓ pint) water
Salt and pepper

Blue cheese croutons:
8 slices of baguette
100 g (3½ oz) dolcelatte cheese

CONVENTIONAL METHOD

1 Put the oil and butter in a large pan set over a low to medium heat. Once the butter has melted, add the onions and cook for 20–25 minutes, stirring frequently. This may seem like a long time, but for this amount of onions you will need it. The onions will turn a lovely golden colour. (Or you can skip this step if you're using the Time Saver Onions.) Add the garlic, herbs (save a few thyme leaves for garnish) and sugar and cook for a further 2–3 minutes. Pour in the vinegar, then add the consommé and water and season well. Cover and cook over the lowest heat possible on your hob for 2–3 hours to give the flavours time to develop and so that the onions turn beautiful and soft.

2 Preheat the oven to 180°C (350°F), Gas Mark 4.

3 To make the croutons, spread the slices of baguette with the blue cheese, then pop onto a baking tray and bake in the oven for 8–10 minutes, until the cheese has melted.

4 To serve, ladle the soup into 4 bowls. Top each bowl with 2 croutons and garnish with a few thyme leaves.

SLOW COOKER METHOD

1 Put the sliced onions in your slow cooker along with the butter, oil and a good pinch of salt and pepper. Stir well, then pop on the lid and cook on the low setting for 12 hours. Alternatively, you can skip this step if you're using Time Saver Onions.

2 Add the rest of the soup ingredients (save a few thyme leaves for garnish) and cook on the low setting for a further 1–2 hours to give the flavours time to develop and so that the onions turn beautiful and soft. Add a splash of water if the onions look like they are catching. Season with salt and pepper.

3 Follow steps 2–4 as above to make the croutons and serve.

TIME SAVER TIP
You could use half a batch of the Time Saver Onions on page 14 instead of the onions listed above.

MUM'S STORE CUPBOARD SAUSAGE CASSEROLE

We used to love sausage casserole as kids. We would arrive home from school to the smell of it ticking away on the stove, more often than not paired with mash (or even Smash – sorry, Mum!). This is a great recipe for using up those cans hanging around in the back of the cupboard. What really makes this for me is that the sausages almost melt in your mouth because they have been cooked for so long. These days I always have a big dollop of fiery English mustard on the side.

SERVES 4

1–2 tablespoons olive oil
8 good-quality pork sausages
1 onion, diced
1 green pepper, diced
2 garlic cloves, crushed
1 teaspoon dried thyme
150 ml (¼ pint) red wine
1 x 400 g (14 oz) can of chopped
    tomatoes
1 x 400 g (14 oz) can of baked beans
300 ml (½ pint) chicken stock if
    using the conventional method
    or 200 ml (⅓ pint) if using the
    slow cooker method
1 tablespoon tomato purée

Chorizo breadcrumbs:
3 tablespoons olive oil
100 g (3½ oz) chorizo sausage, cut
    into very small dice
80 g (2¾ oz) coarse breadcrumbs
2 garlic cloves, crushed

To serve:
Mashed potatoes
English mustard

CONVENTIONAL METHOD

1 Heat the oil in a large heavy-based casserole over a medium heat. Add the sausages and brown for 5–6 minutes, then remove from the casserole and set aside. Add the onion, green pepper, garlic and thyme and cook for around 5 minutes. Pour in the red wine and reduce by half, then add the tomatoes, beans, 300 ml (½ pint) of stock and tomato purée and bring up to a simmer.
2 Return the sausages to the casserole, then cover and cook gently over a low heat for 2 hours.
3 To make the chorizo breadcrumbs, heat the oil in a pan over a medium heat, then add the chorizo and cook for a couple of minutes. Throw in the breadcrumbs and garlic and cook over a low heat for 1 minute.
4 Serve the sausages with a side of your choice (I like mashed potatoes and a dollop of English mustard) and sprinkle over the breadcrumbs.

SLOW COOKER METHOD

1 Follow step 1 as above, then transfer all the ingredients to your slow cooker, making sure you use only 200 ml (⅓ pint) of stock. Cover with the lid and cook on the low setting for 6 hours.
2 Follow steps 3–4 as above.

MOROCCAN CHICKPEA STEW

This is the very essence of a one-pot wonder. If I know I'll be up against the clock in the morning and am going to be out all day, I do my prep the night before and toss all the ingredients into a large sealable freezer bag. In the morning, I just decant all the ingredients into my slow cooker, flick the switch and let the cooker work its magic. I return home to an incredible dinner and it takes only 5 minutes to knock up some couscous to serve with this flavour-packed stew.

SERVES 4

1–2 tablespoons olive oil
1 onion, diced
1 tablespoon tomato purée
1 tablespoon ground cumin
1 heaped teaspoon ground
   coriander
1 teaspoon smoked paprika
1 teaspoon ground cinnamon
1 red pepper, diced
1 x 400 g (14 oz) can of chopped
   tomatoes
2 x 400 g (14 oz) cans of chickpeas,
   drained and rinsed
500 ml (18 fl oz) vegetable stock
100 g (3½ oz) baby spinach
1 tablespoon runny honey
1 tablespoon pomegranate molasses
Salt and pepper
Couscous, to serve

To garnish:
60 g (2¼ oz) flaked almonds, toasted
Seeds from ½ pomegranate

CONVENTIONAL METHOD

1 Heat the oil in a large heavy-based casserole over a low heat. Add the onion and cook for 10 minutes, until golden. Add the tomato purée and spices and cook for a few more minutes, then add the red pepper, tomatoes, chickpeas and stock, then season with salt and pepper. Bring to a simmer, then cover and cook over a low heat for 1 hour.

2 Stir through the spinach and leave it for a minute to wilt, then drizzle in the honey and pomegranate molasses and check for seasoning. Serve with couscous and garnish with the toasted almonds and pomegranate seeds.

SLOW COOKER METHOD

1 Place all the ingredients apart from the spinach, honey and molasses in your slow cooker. Pop on the lid and cook on the low setting for 7 hours.

2 Follow step 2 as above.

BEEF PANTRY PIE

Not every meal is beautifully planned out. Sometimes you have to raid the fridge, cupboards and spice rack for inspiration. We all have that can of soup knocking about at the back of the cupboard, so why not use it as the base for this fantastic slow-cooked beef pie? For those of you who are terrified of using pastry, give a few sheets of scrunched-up filo pastry a try instead of the puff pastry I've used here.

SERVES 4

1–2 tablespoons olive oil

500 g (1 lb 2 oz) skirt steak, cut into 2.5 cm (1 inch) cubes

1 tablespoon plain flour seasoned with salt and pepper

2 Portobello mushrooms, trimmed and sliced

1 onion, diced

2 garlic cloves, crushed

1 x 400g (14 oz) can of oxtail soup

200 ml (⅓ pint) beef stock if using the conventional method or 150 ml (¼ pint) if using the slow cooker method

1 x 300 g (10½ oz) can of new potatoes, drained and diced small

1 tablespoon tomato purée

1 tablespoon Worcestershire sauce

1 teaspoon dried thyme

1 teaspoon English mustard

1 x 375 g (13 oz) pack of shop-bought puff pastry (you will need approx. half of this quantity)

1 egg, beaten

Salt and pepper

CONVENTIONAL METHOD

1 Preheat the oven to 140°C (275°F), Gas Mark 1.

2 Heat a splash of the oil in a large heavy-based casserole over a medium to high heat. Dust the steak in the flour, then add to the casserole and fry until golden, which will take 3–4 minutes. Remove from the casserole and set aside. Add an additional splash of oil and the mushrooms and cook for 6–7 minutes until golden. Add the onion and garlic and continue to cook for a further 3–4 minutes until softened (or add the Time Saver Garlic Base and cook until warmed through).

3 Pour in the soup and 200 ml (⅓ pint) of stock, then stir through the potatoes, tomato purée, Worcestershire sauce, thyme and mustard. Add the steak back to the pot. Cover with a tight-fitting lid and cook in the oven for 4 hours. Season with salt and pepper before transferring to a pie tin. Leave to cool.

4 Increase the oven temperature to 200°C (400°F), Gas Mark 6.

5 Roll out the pastry until it's the thickness of a £1 coin, then cut it into a circle larger than your pie tin. Wet the edges of the tin with a little water, then place the pastry lid on top, crimping down to the edge of the pie dish with the tines of a fork and trimming away any excess pastry (I like to make leaves from the pastry trimmings and put them on top of the pie). Brush with some of the beaten egg, then transfer to the oven and bake for 30–35 minutes, until golden.

SLOW COOKER METHOD

1 Follow step 1 as above.

2 Transfer all the ingredients into your slow cooker, making sure you use only 150 ml (¼ pint) of stock. Cover and cook on the low setting for 6 hours. Season with salt and pepper before transferring to a pie tin.

3 Follow steps 4–5 as above.

TIME SAVER TIP
You could use 1 portion of the Time Saver Garlic Base on page 14 instead of the onion and garlic.

BOURBON BARBECUE CHICKEN ENCHILADAS

I heart enchiladas. Sweet, cheesy, slightly spicy and totally filling, they're one of those proper comforting meals that the whole family will enjoy. I totally love how the inexpensive chicken thighs almost melt down during the slow cooking process but why not try a vegetarian version using extra beans and mushrooms? I've suggested you use shop-bought barbecue sauce but if you want to make your own just follow my recipe on page 82. Serve with some extra cheese and a dollop of cooling soured cream.

SERVES 4

1–2 tablespoons olive oil

6 boneless, skinless chicken thighs, approx. 600 g (1 lb 5 oz)

1 large onion, diced

1 green pepper, sliced

3 garlic cloves, crushed

2 tablespoons bourbon

1 x 400 g (14 oz) can of red kidney beans, drained and rinsed

1 teaspoon ground cumin

½ teaspoon smoked paprika

300 ml (½ pint) chicken stock if using the conventional method or 150 ml (¼ pint) if using the slow cooker method

200 ml (⅓ pint) shop-bought barbecue sauce

8 soft flour tortillas

250 ml (9 fl oz) tomato passata

150 g (5½ oz) Cheddar cheese, grated, plus extra to serve

Salt and pepper

Soured cream, to serve

Fresh coriander, to garnish

CONVENTIONAL METHOD

1 Preheat the oven to 160°C (325°F), Gas Mark 3.

2 Heat the oil in a large heavy-based casserole over a medium to high heat. Add the chicken and fry for 4–5 minutes, until browned.

3 Add the onion, green pepper and garlic and continue to cook for a couple of minutes, until softened. Pour in the bourbon and let it reduce, then add the beans, cumin and paprika. Stir in 300 ml (½ pint) of stock and the barbecue sauce and simmer for a couple of minutes before seasoning with salt and pepper. Cover with a tight-fitting lid, then pop into the oven to cook for 3 hours.

4 Remove the chicken from the casserole and shred it with forks, then add it back to the pot and season with salt and pepper. If you want to thicken the sauce, place the casserole over a medium heat and simmer, uncovered, until reduced.

5 Increase the oven temperature to 190°C (375°F), Gas Mark 5.

6 Spoon some of the chicken mixture onto the centre of a tortilla. Roll it up and place in a large rectangular baking dish. Repeat until all the filling and tortillas are used up to make 8 enchiladas. Pour over the passata in a line lengthways along the centre of the tortillas, then scatter over the grated cheese. Bake in the oven for around 25 minutes, until golden. Serve with some soured cream and garnish with fresh coriander.

SLOW COOKER METHOD

1 If you have time, sear the chicken as in step 2 above until golden because this will add a lot of flavour. Place the chicken, onion, green pepper, garlic, bourbon, beans, spices, 150 ml (¼ pint) of stock and the barbecue sauce into your slow cooker and season with salt and pepper. Pop on the lid and cook on low for 7 hours.

2 Remove the chicken from the slow cooker and shred it with forks, then add it back to the pot and season with salt and pepper.

3 Follow steps 5–6 as above to finish the dish.

CHICKEN AND MUSHROOM MINI POT PIES

Pies are often deemed to be hard work, what with making the filling and then fiddling around with a pastry lid, but I have to say that I really enjoy the step-by-step process of constructing these individual pies. Not only are they creamy and delicious, but they are so simple to make using some store cupboard staples.

SERVES 4

1–2 tablespoons olive oil

4 boneless, skinless chicken thighs, cut into bite-sized pieces

1 tablespoon plain flour

200 g (7 oz) mushrooms of your choice (I like wild, chestnut or enoki), trimmed and sliced

1 onion, very finely diced

2 garlic cloves, crushed

3 thyme sprigs, leaves picked

40 ml (1½ fl oz) brandy

500 ml (18 fl oz) chicken stock if using the conventional method or 200 ml (⅓ pint) boiling chicken stock if using the slow cooker method

150–250 g (5½–9 oz) Maris Piper potatoes, cut into 1 cm (½ inch) cubes

100 ml (3½ fl oz) double cream

70 g (2½ oz) Parmesan cheese, grated

Small handful of chives, chopped

4 sheets of filo pastry

50 g (1¾ oz) butter, melted

Salt and pepper

CONVENTIONAL METHOD

1 Heat the oil in a large heavy-based casserole over a high heat. Dust the chicken in the flour, then add to the casserole and cook for 3–4 minutes, until golden. Remove from the casserole and set aside. Add the mushrooms and fry until golden, which will take 6–7 minutes. Add the onion, garlic and thyme, then reduce the heat to low and cook for around 5 minutes, until softened. Pour in the brandy and let it reduce.

2 Add the 500 ml (18 fl oz) of stock. Add the chicken back in along with the potatoes, then cover with a lid and simmer gently for 1½ hours.

3 Preheat the oven to 180°C (350°F), Gas Mark 4.

4 Take the pot off the heat and stir through the cream, Parmesan and chives. Season with salt and pepper.

5 Using four 16 cm (6¼ inch) oblong enamel pie dishes, fill them with the chicken and mushroom mixture. Put a scrunched-up sheet of filo pastry on top of each dish, then brush with the melted butter. Bake in the oven for 20–25 minutes, until golden brown.

SLOW COOKER METHOD

1 Follow step 1 as above.

2 Transfer the chicken and the mushroom mixture to your slow cooker along with the 200 ml (⅓ pint) of boiling stock and the potatoes and season with salt and pepper. Put the lid on and cook on the low setting for 6 hours.

3 Follow steps 3–5 as above.

LAZY MEXICAN CHICKEN LASAGNE

A firm family favourite. There's no worry about cooking any pasta as I use flour tortillas and while I've used chicken breasts here thighs would also work well. If anyone doesn't like the chilli kick of Mexicana cheese, just replace it with a crumbly mature Cheddar.

SERVES 4

1–2 tablespoons olive oil

3 boneless, skinless chicken breasts, cut into small chunks

1 onion, very finely diced

1 green pepper, diced

1 red pepper, diced

4 garlic cloves, crushed

2 tablespoons tomato purée

1 x 400 g (14 oz) can of red kidney beans, drained and rinsed

600 ml (20 fl oz) chicken stock if using the conventional method or 400 ml (14 fl oz) if using the slow cooker method

2 teaspoons dried oregano

1 heaped teaspoon smoked paprika

1 teaspoon ground cumin

3 flour tortillas, use rectangular ones or cut down round ones

1 small bag of cheese-flavoured tortilla chips, crushed

Salt and pepper

Side salad, to serve

White sauce:

80 g (2¾ oz) unsalted butter

80 g (2¾ oz) plain flour

800–900 ml (28–32 fl oz) milk

150 g (5½ oz) Mexicana Cheddar cheese, grated

CONVENTIONAL METHOD

1 Heat a splash of the oil in a large pan over a medium to high heat. Add the chicken and brown for 5–6 minutes. Remove from the pan and set aside. Add another splash of oil, then add the onion, green and red peppers and garlic and cook for 5 minutes, until softened. Stir through the tomato purée, then return the chicken to the pan along with the beans, 600 ml (20 fl oz) of stock and the oregano, smoked paprika and cumin. Reduce the heat to a simmer and cook for 20 minutes, then season with a pinch of salt and pepper.

2 To make the white sauce, melt the butter in a pan over a medium heat, then whisk in the flour and cook for 2 minutes. Gradually pour in 800 ml (28 fl oz) of the milk while whisking and continue whisking until it comes to a boil, then reduce the heat and simmer for 5 minutes, stirring occasionally. Add the remaining milk if needed to get a loose consistency. Season with salt and pepper, then add half of the cheese and stir until melted.

3 Preheat the oven to 200°C (400°F), Gas Mark 6. Grease a lasagne dish with a little oil.

4 Assemble the lasagne in the greased dish by alternately layering the chicken mixture, white sauce and tortillas, creating 3 layers and finishing with the white sauce. Scatter over the remaining cheese and the crushed tortilla chips, then cook in the oven for 30 minutes. Leave to stand for 5 minutes, then cut into portions and serve with a crisp side salad.

SLOW COOKER METHOD

1 Follow step 1 as above or put the chicken, veg, tomato purée, beans, 400 ml (14 fl oz) of stock, the spices and a pinch of salt and pepper in your slow cooker. Cover and cook on the low setting for 4 hours.

2 Follow step 2 as above.

3 If you've used the slow cooker in step 1, then transfer the chicken filling to a bowl, clean out the slow cooker pot and grease it with a little oil. Assemble the lasagne in your greased slow cooker by alternately layering the chicken mixture, white sauce and tortillas (cut or tear the tortillas to fit the pot), creating 3 layers and finishing with the white sauce. Scatter over the remaining cheese, then cover and cook on the low setting for 4 hours.

4 Leave to stand for 5 minutes, then sprinkle with the crushed tortilla chips and cut into portions. Serve with a crisp side salad.

SLOW-ROASTED BLOODY MARY PASTA SAUCE

Slow-roasted tomatoes are one of my favourite things to eat. By cooking them gently and drying them out, you intensify the flavour tenfold. This beats any shop-bought pasta sauce hands down, and best of all you can double the recipe and freeze portions until needed, giving you a meal in minutes because all the work has been done for you in your oven or slow cooker beforehand.

SERVES 8

12 large ripe plum tomatoes
2 tablespoons olive oil, plus extra
    for cooking
2 tablespoons balsamic vinegar
3 garlic cloves, crushed
1 heaped teaspoon dried oregano
1 onion, finely diced
1 tablespoon tomato purée
100 g (3½ oz) black olives, pitted
    and halved
2 tablespoons Worcestershire sauce
2 tablespoons vodka
1 teaspoon caster sugar
1 teaspoon Tabasco sauce
200 ml (⅓ pint) water
250 g (9 oz) linguine pasta
Salt and pepper
Parmesan cheese, for grating
Fresh basil, to garnish

CONVENTIONAL METHOD

1 Preheat the oven to 140°C (275°F), Gas Mark 1.

2 Cut a cross into the base of each tomato, then pop into a large pan of boiling water for 1 minute. Remove from the water with a slotted spoon and plunge into a bowl of ice water, then peel the skins away and cut each tomato in half.

3 Place the tomato halves on a baking tray, cut side up, then drizzle with the 2 tablespoons of olive oil and the balsamic vinegar, garlic and oregano. Season with a pinch of salt and pepper. Toss them around to make sure they are well coated, then make sure they're all cut side up again and roast in the oven for 2 hours.

4 Meanwhile, heat a splash of oil in a pan over a medium heat. Add the onion and gently cook for 5 minutes, then add the tomato purée and cook for a further minute. Pop into a blender along with the roasted tomatoes and blitz together. Pass through a fine mesh sieve into a clean pan, then add the olives, Worcestershire sauce, vodka, sugar, Tabasco sauce and a good pinch of salt and pepper. Simmer very gently for 10 minutes. Add enough of the water to get your desired sauce consistency.

5 Cook the pasta according to the packet instructions, then drain and toss through the pasta sauce. Finish with a good grating of Parmesan cheese and garnish with fresh basil.

SLOW COOKER METHOD

1 You have to follow the oven method in steps 1–3 as for the conventional method opposite in order to dry out the tomatoes and intensify the flavour.

2 While the tomatoes are cooking, pop the onion into your slow cooker along with a splash of oil and cook on the low setting for 2 hours.

3 Add the roasted tomatoes along with the rest of the ingredients apart from the olives and pasta and cook for 2 hours. Leave to cool slightly, then transfer to a blender and blitz until smooth. Stir in the olives, then season with salt and pepper. Add some extra water if needed to get your desired sauce consistency.

4 Follow step 5 as for the conventional method opposite.

Feasts for Friends

Many of these recipes were born from my childhood memories of enjoying food with my family and friends. I vividly remember the weekly visits to go see my Nanny Fran. On opening the door, I'd be hit full on by an incredible heady aroma of spices, as my nan always had a huge pot of her famous Cape Malay chicken curry on the hob. It was at that point that food always brought me to a place where I was happy.

There really is something for everyone in this chapter, from the Festive Soda-baked Ham served with homemade chips and pickles on Boxing Day to a gooey Cheese Fondue with Garlic Tear 'n' Share Loaf, and not forgetting Nanny Fran's Chicken Curry. Got an extra large crowd to feed? These recipes can be easily doubled or tripled, so long as you have enough space in your oven for a few roasting tins, a big enough casserole, or more than one slow cooker. So try some of these and capture that feeling I had as a child and still do to this day.

CHEESE FONDUE WITH GARLIC TEAR 'N' SHARE LOAF

This is a cheese lover's dream right here, and best of all you don't need a special fondue pot to make it – go ahead and make it right in your slow cooker. I've used a combination of nutty Gruyère and mature Cheddar cheese, but feel free to experiment – a little Stilton crumbled through it is delicious too. My tear 'n' share loaf is perfect for dipping in the fondue, but I also like to have some pickles on hand to cut through the richness of the cheese.

SERVES 4

1 garlic clove, halved
200 ml (⅓ pint) dry white wine
300 g (10½ oz) mature Cheddar cheese
300 g (10½ oz) Gruyère cheese
1 heaped teaspoon cornflour
2 rosemary sprigs
Pickles, to serve

Garlic tear 'n' share loaf:
1 large round or oval loaf of bread
90 g (3¼ oz) salted butter, melted
5 garlic cloves, crushed
2 tablespoons finely chopped parsley

CONVENTIONAL METHOD

1 Preheat the oven to 160°C (325°F), Gas Mark 3.
2 Rub a heatproof bowl with the halved garlic clove, then discard it. Set this bowl over a pan of simmering water, then pour in the wine and heat gently.
3 Grate the cheeses into a separate large bowl, then sprinkle in the cornflour and toss well to coat the cheese. Add the cheese to the wine a handful at a time, stirring until melted. Once it's silky-smooth, I like to add the whole rosemary sprigs to let them gently infuse. You can add a little more wine to loosen the fondue to your desired consistency if necessary.
4 To make the tear 'n' share loaf, cut the bread at 2.5 cm (1 inch) intervals in a diamond pattern, being careful not to cut all the way through. Mix the melted butter, garlic and parsley together in a bowl, then brush this in between the cuts in the loaf. Place the bread on a baking tray and cover with foil, then pop into the oven to bake for 12 minutes. Remove from the oven and pull the foil back to expose the bread, then bake, uncovered, for a further 10 minutes, until golden.
5 To serve, pull the bread apart and dip it into the gooey fondue. Serve with pickles on the side.

SLOW COOKER METHOD

1 Pour the wine into a small saucepan and bring up to a simmer. Rub the slow cooker pot with the halved garlic clove, then discard it. Put your slow cooker on the low setting, then pour in the wine.

2 Grate the cheeses into a separate large bowl, then sprinkle in the cornflour and toss well to coat the cheese. Add the cheese to the wine a handful at a time, stirring until melted. Once it's silky-smooth, I like to add the whole rosemary sprigs to let them gently infuse. Pop the lid on and set to warm for 1 hour, stirring every 20 minutes. You can add a little more wine to loosen the fondue to your desired consistency if necessary.

3 Follow steps 4–5 as for the conventional method opposite.

TIP

This is a great recipe for using up all those cheeses you buy during the festive season.

WHOLE SLOW COOKER CHICKEN

To brine or not to brine, that is the question. Well, my answer to that would be a resounding yes! Brining simply means soaking the chicken in salty water, but it makes such a difference to the flavour and tenderness of the bird. Give it a go, but of course if you don't have time you can skip this step.

SERVES 4

1 whole chicken, approx. 1.5 kg
   (3 lb 5 oz)
1 lemon, halved

Brining liquid:
120 g (4¼ oz) salt
60 g (2¼ oz) caster sugar
2 litres (3½ pints) water

Spice rub:
1 heaped teaspoon dried thyme
1 teaspoon onion powder
1 teaspoon garlic powder
1 heaped teaspoon sea salt flakes
1 teaspoon ground black pepper

To serve:
Your usual Sunday roast trimmings

CONVENTIONAL METHOD

1 To make the brine, place the salt, sugar and water in a large pan and bring to a boil, stirring to dissolve the salt and sugar. It is important to leave the brine to cool completely before continuing with this step. Place the chicken in a large ziplock freezer bag or plastic container, then pour in the cooled brine until the chicken is covered. Seal tightly before placing in the refrigerator overnight.
2 The next day, preheat the oven to 190°C (375°F), Gas Mark 5.
3 Mix all the spice rub ingredients together and set aside.
4 Remove the chicken from the brine and thoroughly pat it dry with kitchen paper, then you're ready to cook.
5 Stuff the lemon halves inside the chicken cavity, then rub the chicken liberally with the spice mix. Place the chicken on a trivet set within a roasting tin, then roast in the oven for 45 minutes per 1 kg (2 lb 4 oz) plus 20 minutes. A 1.5 kg (3 lb 5 oz) chicken should take about 1½ hours to cook. The chicken is ready when the juices run clear when a skewer is inserted into the thickest part.
6 Remove the chicken from the oven. Cover loosely with foil and allow to rest for at least 20 minutes before carving. Serve with your usual Sunday roast trimmings, such as potatoes, carrots and cabbage.

SLOW COOKER METHOD

1 Follow steps 1, 3 and 4 as for the conventional method opposite.
2 Stuff the lemon halves inside the chicken cavity, then rub the chicken liberally
   with the spice mix. Place the chicken on top of a trivet within your slow cooker
   (if you don't have a trivet, see my tip below). Put on the lid and cook on the low
   setting for 7 hours. If you want to crisp up the skin, you can put the chicken in
   a hot oven for 10–15 minutes at the end.
3 Carve the chicken and serve with your usual Sunday roast trimmings, such
   as potatoes, carrots and cabbage.

TIP

To make a trivet for your slow cooker, scrunch up some foil into golf ball-sized
pieces. This will help keep the chicken from stewing in the juices collecting in the
bottom of the pot during the prolonged cooking period. You can make a delicious
gravy from these cooking juices so don't throw them away.

MY CELEBRATION TWO-DAY PORK BELLY

This is my special occasion dish. By cooking it slowly, you gently render out all the fat and end up with the most delicious, tender pork belly you will ever eat. As a bonus, you'll have already made your sauce to go with this out of your braising liquid. Served with the crispy crackling and some apple sauce on the side, special meals or Sunday dinners will never be the same again.

SERVES 4

1–2 tablespoons olive oil
1 kg (2 lb 4 oz) boneless pork belly, skin removed and set aside
1 onion, roughly diced
1 carrot, diced
2 celery sticks, diced
2 garlic cloves, chopped
3 thyme sprigs
1 tablespoon fennel seeds
600 ml (20 fl oz) chicken stock
500 ml (18 fl oz) scrumpy or dry cider
Butter, for frying
Salt and pepper

To serve:
Maple roasted parsnips
Sautéed cavolo nero
Apple sauce

CONVENTIONAL METHOD

1 Heat the oil in a pan that's large enough to hold the pork. Add the onion, carrot, celery, garlic, thyme and fennel seeds and fry over a medium heat for around 5 minutes. Pour in the stock and the cider and add a good pinch of salt and pepper. Add the pork belly and bring to a simmer. Cover with a lid and braise gently for 3 hours.

2 Remove the pork belly and place it on a baking tray lined with foil, then place another tray on top. Weigh it down to compress the pork, then wrap everything in clingfilm. Place in the refrigerator to chill overnight.

3 Strain the braising liquid into a container, then cover and place that in the refrigerator overnight too.

4 The next day, preheat the oven to 200°C (400°F), Gas Mark 6.

5 For perfect crackling, score the pork belly skin with a very sharp knife. Season with salt and pepper and place it in between two baking trays. Roast in the oven for 40–50 minutes, until crispy.

6 While the crackling is cooking, cut the pork belly into 4 portions and fry in some butter or oil in a frying pan over a low to medium heat for 12–15 minutes, until golden and warmed through. Leave to rest for 10 minutes.

7 Meanwhile, prepare the sauce. Scrape away the fat that will have solidified on top of the braising liquid and discard it. Return the liquid to a pan and reduce over a high heat until slightly thickened.

8 Serve the golden pork belly with the crackling, maple roasted parsnips, sautéed cavolo nero or other seasonal greens, apple sauce and finally a good splash of the reduced sauce.

SLOW COOKER METHOD

1 Place the stock and cider in a large saucepan over a high heat. Bring to a boil.

2 Add the vegetables, garlic, thyme and fennel seeds to the slow cooker. Pour in the boiling liquid and season with salt and pepper. Add the pork belly, making sure it's covered by the liquid. Put on the lid and cook on low for 7 hours.

3 Follow steps 2–8 as above.

FESTIVE SODA-BAKED HAM

I love the family food sharing experience through the festive period, but nothing comes close to Boxing Day cold meat and pickles with homemade chips. This salty baked ham is offset beautifully by the sweet, sticky glaze. You can use whatever fizzy drink you like, so experiment with your flavour combinations – try cola, cherry cola or ginger beer. Just don't use a sugar-free soda, otherwise it won't reduce down to a syrup. If you want to live a little dangerously, add some dried chilli flakes to the glaze.

SERVES 12

2 kg (4 lb 8 oz) boneless
    unsmoked gammon joint
2 onions, sliced
1 large carrot, chopped
1 bouquet garni (rosemary,
    bay, thyme)
1 cinnamon stick
1 star anise
1 teaspoon black peppercorns
500 ml (18 fl oz) cloudy apple juice
500 ml (18 fl oz) cider
Cloves, for studding the ham

Glaze:
600 ml (20 fl oz) dandelion
    and burdock soda
Juice of 1 lime
1 teaspoon English mustard

To serve:
Oven chips
Pickles

CONVENTIONAL METHOD

1 Place the gammon in a large pan along with the vegetables, bouquet garni and spices. Pour in the apple juice, cider and enough water to cover the gammon. Bring to a simmer, then cook gently for around 1½ hours. Leave to cool in the pot.
2 Preheat the oven to 200°C (400°F), Gas Mark 6.
3 Lift the ham from the pot and place on a cutting board. Remove the skin from the joint, then score the fat in a diamond pattern. Stud the ham with a clove where the cuts cross.
4 To make the glaze, pour the soda into a saucepan and bring to the boil over a high heat until reduced, thickened and syrupy, then stir through the lime juice and mustard. Brush the ham liberally with the glaze, then bake in the oven for 30 minutes.
5 Rest for at least 20 minutes before carving. Serve with oven chips and pickles.

SLOW COOKER METHOD

1 Place the onions and carrot in the bottom of your slow cooker. Place the gammon on top, then pour in the apple juice and cider. Add the bouquet garni and spices, then put the lid on and cook on the low setting for 8 hours.
2 Follow steps 2–5 as above.

TIP

To work out the cooking time for your gammon, allow 20 minutes per 450 g (1 lb) plus 20 minutes. A 2 kg (4 lb 8 oz) gammon joint will take 1 hour 50 minutes to cook.

ZESTY LAMB KLEFTIKO

Tired of your traditional Sunday roast? Then give this slow-cooked Greek lamb a try. If you have a smaller slow cooker, then replace the whole lamb shoulder with a couple of smaller lamb rump joints or a boned and rolled shoulder – the flavour will be incredible either way.

SERVES 4

1 lamb shoulder, approx. 1.5 kg (3 lb 5 oz)

1–2 tablespoons olive oil (slow cooker method only)

800 g (1 lb 12 oz) waxy potatoes (such as Desiree), quartered

2 onions, thinly sliced

100 ml (3½ fl oz) white wine if using the conventional method or 50 ml (2 fl oz) if using the slow cooker method

100 ml (3½ fl oz) lamb stock if using the conventional method or 50 ml (2 fl oz) if using the slow cooker method

Salt and pepper

Marinade:

6 garlic cloves, crushed

1 bay leaf

Juice of 1 lemon

Zest of ½ lemon

1 tablespoon dried oregano

1 teaspoon chopped rosemary

½ teaspoon ground cinnamon

To serve:

Raita

Feta cheese, crumbled

CONVENTIONAL METHOD

1 Combine all the marinade ingredients together. Poke holes in the lamb with the tip of a sharp knife, then rub the marinade into the lamb, making sure you work it into the little pockets you have created. Put into a large sealable bag and place in the refrigerator overnight.

2 Preheat the oven to 160°C (325°F), Gas Mark 3.

3 Lay 2 long pieces of foil, one horizontally and then one vertically to form a cross, inside a large roasting tin. Repeat with 2 long pieces of nonstick baking paper. Place the potatoes and onions in the centre of the cross, then pop the lamb on top and season with salt and pepper. Pour in the 100 ml (3½ fl oz) of wine and stock. Bring each piece of baking paper up and over the lamb, tucking in each end to form a sort of parcel. Finally, pull the foil up over the lamb and scrunch the ends together to seal tightly. Cook in the oven for 4 hours.

4 Remove from the oven and turn the heat up to 200°C (400°F), Gas Mark 6. Open the parcel and scrunch the foil and the baking paper down the sides of the tin. Return to the oven for 20–25 minutes to give the lamb a lovely golden colour.

5 Carve into slices and serve with some minty raita and crumbled feta.

SLOW COOKER METHOD

1 Follow step 1 as above.

2 Season the lamb, then sear in a hot pan with a splash of oil until golden. Place the potatoes and onions in your slow cooker, then pour in the 50 ml (2 fl oz) of wine and stock and place the lamb on top. Put the lid on and cook on the low setting for 7 hours.

3 Remove the lid, lift the crock pot from your slow cooker and place it under a hot grill to brown the lamb (check that your crock pot is grill suitable first).

4 Follow step 5 as above.

BEEF BOURGUIGNON

This take on a traditional recipe is a great one to keep ticking over until you're ready to eat. There's a very good reason this dish has become a French classic: it's rich, indulgent and incredibly tasty. Most recipes call for a whole bottle of wine, but I've reduced the amount because I find it too rich with a full bottle – well, that and the fact that I like to save a couple of glasses to enjoy with the meal!

SERVES 4

1–2 tablespoons olive oil

2 ox cheeks, approx. 900 g (2 lb)

1 heaped tablespoon plain flour
seasoned with salt and pepper

100 g (3½ oz) smoked pancetta
lardons

1 tablespoon tomato purée

250 ml (9 fl oz) red wine

100 ml (3½ fl oz) beef stock

200 g (7 oz) baby carrots, halved
lengthways

12 baby onions or shallots,
peeled (see the tip)

A few thyme sprigs

1 bay leaf

To serve:
Mashed potatoes
Dijon mustard

CONVENTIONAL METHOD

1 Preheat the oven to 160°C (325°F), Gas Mark 3.

2 Heat the oil in a large heavy-based casserole over a medium to high heat. Cut each ox cheek in half so that you have 4 portions in total, then dust with the seasoned flour. Add to the casserole and brown for 3–4 minutes, until golden. Remove from the pot and set aside.

3 Add the pancetta and fry for 3–4 minutes, until golden, then add the tomato purée and cook for a further minute. Pour in the wine and stock and bring up to a simmer.

4 Add the carrots and baby onions or shallots to the pot along with the ox cheeks, then add the thyme and bay leaf. Give it a quick stir, then pop on a tight-fitting lid and cook in the oven for 3 hours. Check halfway through the cooking time to gently turn the cheeks and add a little water if required.

5 Serve with a creamy mash and some mustard on the side.

SLOW COOKER METHOD

1 Follow steps 2–3 as for the conventional method opposite.
2 Pop the carrots and baby onions or shallots into the slow cooker along with the ox cheeks, thyme and bay leaf and the contents of the casserole. Stir to make sure everything is well combined. Put on the lid and cook on the low setting for 7 hours.
3 Follow step 5 as for the conventional method opposite.

TIP

To peel baby onions or shallots, put them in a pot of boiling water for 30 seconds. Drain and pop into a bowl of ice water until they're cool enough to handle, then cut off the root end and squeeze the onions out of their skins.

NANNY FRAN'S CHICKEN CURRY

One of my earliest memories is visiting Nanny Fran who always had a pot of this on the go. As soon as you walked in, you were hit by the aroma of deep spice. We loved the chicken skin, which often didn't even make it to the plate. You can remove it before cooking, but it adds bags of flavour.

SERVES 4

1–2 tablespoons olive oil
4–6 large chicken thighs, bone in and
    skin on
2 large onions, sliced
6 garlic cloves, crushed
1 thumb-sized piece of fresh root ginger
1 red chilli, deseeded and finely sliced
1 cinnamon stick
1 star anise
1 heaped tablespoon tomato purée
1 x 500 g (1 lb 2 oz) carton of tomato
    passata
500 g (1 lb 2 oz) Maris Piper potatoes,
    quartered
500 ml (18 fl oz) chicken stock if using
    the conventional method or 200 ml
    (⅓ pint) if using the slow cooker
    method
Salt and pepper
Fresh coriander, to garnish (optional)

Spice mix:
4 cloves
3 cardamom pods
1 tablespoon fennel seeds
1 teaspoon nigella seeds
1 teaspoon mustard seeds
1 tablespoon garam masala
1 teaspoon ground turmeric

TIME SAVER TIP
You could use 2 portions of the Time Saver Curry Base on page 14 instead of the onions, garlic and ginger.

CONVENTIONAL METHOD

1 Heat the oil in a large pan over a medium heat. Add the chicken thighs and brown for 3–4 minutes, until golden. Remove from the pan and set aside.

2 Add the onions, garlic, ginger (or Time Saver Curry Base), chilli, cinnamon stick and star anise and cook over a low to medium heat for 10–15 minutes, until the onions are soft and golden. Take your time at this stage.

3 Meanwhile, grind up the whole spices for the spice mix in a pestle and mortar, then add these to the pan along with the other spices and cook for 1–2 minutes. Stir through the tomato purée and cook for another minute or two.

4 Add the passata, potatoes and 500 ml (18 fl oz) of stock, then add the chicken back in along with a pinch of salt and pepper. Bring up to a simmer, then cover and cook over the lowest possible heat for 3 hours.

5 Remove the lid and cook until the sauce has thickened and the potatoes are cooked through. This might take 20–30 minutes. Garnish with fresh coriander (if using).

SLOW COOKER METHOD

1 Follow steps 1–3 as above.

2 Spoon the onion mixture into your slow cooker, then add the passata, potatoes and 200 ml (⅓ pint) of stock. Add the chicken too along with a pinch of salt and pepper. Pop the lid on and cook on the low setting for 6 hours. Garnish with fresh coriander (if using).

FANTASTIC FISH PIE

I was brought up on classic fish pie. I remember coming home from school, the entire house humming from the smoked fish, which was usually bright yellow haddock poaching in milk on the stovetop. I could smell it for days afterwards. Feel free to use smoked fish in this, but I leave it out these days. The pie also contained eggs, which are an inexpensive way to bulk out the filling. If I'm honest this one does work better the conventional way in the oven because you'll get that crispy topping associated with a fish pie.

SERVES 4

1–2 tablespoons olive oil

1 leek, shredded

500 g (1 lb 2 oz) selection of fish (I like salmon, haddock and pollock), cut into 2.5 cm (1 inch) cubes

3 eggs, hard-boiled, shelled and quartered

100 g (3½ oz) Cheddar cheese, grated

Salt and pepper

Buttered spinach, to serve

Béchamel:

50 g (1¾ oz) unsalted butter

50 g (1¾ oz) plain flour

400–500 ml (14–18 fl oz) milk

2 tablespoons chopped flat leaf parsley

1 teaspoon Dijon mustard

Topping:

800 g (1 lb 12 oz) Maris Piper potatoes, peeled and cubed

30 g (1 oz) unsalted butter

80 ml (2¾ fl oz) warmed milk

CONVENTIONAL METHOD

1 Preheat the oven to 200°C (400°F), Gas Mark 6.
2 To make the béchamel (white sauce), melt the butter in a pan over a medium heat, then whisk in the flour and cook for 2–3 minutes. Gradually pour in the milk and continue whisking until the sauce is thickened and smooth. Use enough milk to get a loose consistency. Add the parsley and mustard, then season with salt and pepper. Set aside.
3 Heat the oil in a frying pan over a medium heat. Add the shredded leek and fry for 5 minutes, then place in a bowl along with the fish, eggs and white sauce and stir in half the cheese. Gently fold everything together, then season with salt and pepper. Pour the mixture into a pie tin or baking dish.
4 Boil the peeled potatoes for 15 minutes, until cooked through, then drain and mash until smooth with the butter and milk and season with salt and pepper. Top the fish with the mashed potatoes, then run a fork across the top to give it some texture and sprinkle over the remaining grated cheese.
5 Bake in the oven for 30 minutes, until golden. Serve with some buttered spinach on the side.

SLOW COOKER METHOD

1 Follow steps 2–3 as above.
2 Grease your slow cooker pot, then spoon in the fish pie mix. Pop the lid on and cook on the high setting for 1 hour.
3 Meanwhile, make the topping. Boil the peeled potatoes for 15 minutes, until cooked through, then drain and mash until smooth with the butter and milk and season with salt and pepper. Top the fish with the mashed potatoes, then run the tines of a fork across the top to give it some texture and sprinkle over the remaining grated cheese. Put the lid back on and cook for a further 30 minutes.

SLOW-ROASTED LAMB WITH BOULANGÈRE POTATOES

One of my inspirations for writing this book are the memories created by food – not only the eating of it, but the bringing together of family and friends. This recipe is the perfect sharing dish and brings back memories of a holiday in Cornwall with the Edwards family when I was 10. My Uncle Ed cooked this for us one evening and I was truly gobsmacked at how incredible it tasted. I think it may have been the first time I had tasted fresh herbs, but the simple combo of slow-roasted lamb, garlic and rosemary will stay with me forever.

SERVES 4

1 lamb shoulder, approx. 1.2 kg
    (2 lb 10 oz)
4 garlic cloves, thickly sliced
5 rosemary sprigs
1–2 tablespoons olive oil (slow
    cooker method only)
800 g (1 lb 12 oz) Maris Piper
    potatoes, thinly sliced
2 onions, thinly sliced
Small bunch of thyme
30 g (1 oz) unsalted butter, melted
300 ml (½ pint) hot chicken stock
    if using the conventional method
    or 200 ml (⅓ pint) boiling chicken
    stock if using the slow cooker
    method
Salt and pepper
Seasonal greens, to serve

CONVENTIONAL METHOD

1 Preheat the oven to 200°C (400°F), Gas Mark 6.
2 Using the tip of a sharp knife, make pockets all over the lamb and stud each one with a slice of garlic and some rosemary, making sure you push them right in.
3 Scatter a layer of potato slices on a roasting tin, then add some onions, a sprinkling of fresh thyme leaves and a pinch of salt and pepper. Repeat until all the potatoes and onions have been used up.
4 Stir together the melted butter and 300 ml (½ pint) of stock, then pour this over the potatoes and onions and place the lamb shoulder on top. Cook in the oven for 20 minutes, then cover the tray with foil, reduce the temperature to 160°C (325°F), Gas Mark 3 and cook for a further 4 hours.
5 Leave to rest for 20 minutes under the foil before carving. Before serving you can spoon off some of the fat that has rendered from the lamb. Carve the lamb into slices and serve with seasonal greens.

SLOW COOKER METHOD

1 Using the tip of a sharp knife, make pockets all over the lamb and stud each one with a slice of garlic and some rosemary, making sure you push them right in. Heat the oil in a large pan over a medium heat, then add the lamb and sear for 7–8 minutes, until golden on all sides.
2 Scatter a layer of potato slices in the slow cooker, then add some onions, a sprinkling of fresh thyme leaves and a pinch of salt and pepper. Repeat until all the potatoes and onions have been used up.
3 Stir together the melted butter and 200 ml (⅓ pint) of boiling stock, then pour this over the potatoes and onions and place the lamb shoulder on top. Cover with the lid and cook on the low setting for 8 hours.
4 Remove the lid, lift the crock pot from your slow cooker and place it under a hot grill to brown the lamb (check that your crock pot is grill suitable first). Carve the lamb into slices and serve with some seasonal greens.

MIDDLE EASTERN SPICED LAMB FLATBREADS

This is an incredible sharing meal, one you can just plonk on the table for a DIY assembly job – the sort of food that brings family and friends together. I love to cook lamb this way, spiced with one of my favourite ingredients, rose harissa. Its punchy chilli heat and floral notes really stand up against the rich slow-cooked lamb.

SERVES 4

3 garlic cloves, crushed

1 tablespoon finely grated fresh root ginger

1 heaped teaspoon rose harissa paste

1 teaspoon ground cinnamon

1 teaspoon ground cumin

1 teaspoon ground turmeric

Juice of ½ lemon

1 lamb shoulder approx. 1.2 kg (2 lb 10 oz)

300 ml (½ pint) water if using the conventional method or 100 ml (3½ fl oz) boiling water if using the slow cooker method

Salt and pepper

Harissa yogurt:
100 ml (3½ fl oz) natural yogurt

1 teaspoon rose harissa paste

To serve:
4 round flatbreads

1 small tub of hummus

Seeds from ½ pomegranate

60 g (2¼ oz) toasted pine nuts

Small mint leaves

CONVENTIONAL METHOD

1 Combine the garlic, ginger, harissa, spices and lemon juice, then rub this all over the lamb joint. Cover and marinate in the refrigerator for 24 hours.
2 Preheat the oven to 160°C (325°F), Gas Mark 3.
3 Place the lamb on a rack set inside a roasting tin and season with salt and pepper. Pour in the 300 ml (½ pint) of water, then cover tightly with a large piece of foil and cook in the oven for 4 hours.
4 Crank the oven up to 220°C (425°F), Gas Mark 7, then remove the foil and cook for 20 minutes more. Remove from the oven and leave to rest for at least 20 minutes before pulling the lamb into bite-sized chunks.
5 Pour the yogurt into a bowl, then marble the harissa through with a spoon, ready to drizzle over the finished dish. Keep refrigerated until needed.
6 Warm the flatbreads, then spread with hummus. Add some lamb, then top with pomegranate seeds, toasted pine nuts, mint leaves and a drizzle of the harissa yogurt.

SLOW COOKER METHOD

1 Follow step 1 as above.
2 Place the lamb in your slow cooker on top of a trivet and season with salt and pepper. (If you don't have a trivet, see the tip on page 169.) Pour in the 100 ml (3½ fl oz) of boiling water, then put on the lid and cook on the low setting for 8 hours.
3 I like to crisp up the lamb in a hot oven set at 220°C (425°F), Gas Mark 7, uncovered, for 20 minutes, then let it rest for at least 20 minutes before pulling into bite-sized chunks.
4 Follow steps 5–6 as above.

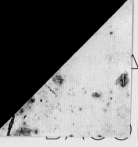

...ALO PULLED CHICKEN
... BLUE CHEESE AND
...ON SLAW

If you fancy a change from pulled pork, then my Buffalo pulled chicken might be just the thing. The chicken is so tender that it falls apart and it's coated in a punchy Buffalo sauce. I've paired this with a crunchy blue cheese slaw and the classic combo is an absolute dream. It's a great summer dish to enjoy in the garden when you can't be bothered to fire up the barbecue.

SERVES 4

6 large boneless, skinless chicken
  thighs, approx. 600 g (1 lb 5 oz)
1 onion, sliced
150 ml (¼ pint) Buffalo hot sauce
  (I like Frank's RedHot)
2 tablespoons tomato ketchup
1 tablespoon runny honey
1 heaped teaspoon garlic powder
Brioche rolls, toasted, to serve

Blue cheese and bacon slaw:
100 g (3½ oz) smoked pancetta
  lardons
¼ white cabbage, cored and
  shredded
1 red onion, very thinly sliced
100 g (3½ oz) blue cheese, crumbled
3 tablespoons mayonnaise
1 heaped teaspoon wholegrain
  mustard
Salt and pepper

CONVENTIONAL METHOD

1 Preheat the oven to 160°C (325°F), Gas Mark 3.
2 Place the chicken thighs in a baking dish with the onion, hot sauce, ketchup, honey and garlic powder. Stir well, then cover tightly with a double layer of foil and cook in the oven for 3 hours.
3 Remove from the oven and use forks to shred the chicken, then add it back to the sauce. Add a little boiling water if you want to make it saucier.
4 Meanwhile, to make the slaw, fry off the pancetta in a hot, dry pan for 3–4 minutes, until crispy, then remove from the pan with a slotted spoon and set aside to cool on a plate lined with kitchen paper. Combine the cabbage, onion, blue cheese and pancetta in a bowl and toss to combine, then add the mayonnaise and mustard, season with salt and pepper and toss to combine.
5 Divide the pulled chicken between the toasted rolls and top with a good helping of the slaw.

SLOW COOKER METHOD

1 Pop the chicken, onion, hot sauce, ketchup, honey and garlic powder into your slow cooker. Cover with the lid and cook on the low setting for 6 hours.
2 Remove the chicken from the slow cooker and shred using forks, then add it back to the sauce.
3 Follow steps 4–5 as above.

TEAR 'N' SHARE SLOPPY JOE SLIDER BAKE

I'm not sure why this much-loved American classic hasn't hit it off over here in the UK. What's not to love about mounds of spiced minced beef in a sandwich, topped with one of my guilty pleasures, processed cheese? I love the sharing nature of this dish – bring it straight to the table, tear off a slider and prepare to get messy! The kids will love this one.

SERVES 4

1–2 tablespoons olive oil
500 g (1 lb 2 oz) minced beef
1 large onion, finely diced
1 green pepper, finely diced
1 garlic clove, crushed
500 ml (18 fl oz) beef stock if
    using the conventional method
    or 200 ml (⅓ pint) if using the
    slow cooker method
3 tablespoons tomato ketchup
3 tablespoons Worcestershire sauce
2 tablespoons sweet chilli sauce
1 tablespoon tomato purée
1 tablespoon red wine vinegar
1 x 12 pack of slider buns, snack
    rolls or small soft round rolls
12 processed cheese slices
Salt and pepper

Garlic butter:
80 g (2¾ oz) salted butter, melted
3 garlic cloves, crushed
2 tablespoons finely chopped
    parsley (optional)

To serve:
Oven chips
Creamy coleslaw

CONVENTIONAL METHOD

1 Heat the oil in a large pan over a high heat. Add the minced beef and fry for 7–8 minutes, until nicely browned. Add the onion, green pepper and garlic and cook for a further 5 minutes. Add the 500 ml (18 fl oz) of stock and the ketchup, Worcestershire sauce, sweet chilli sauce, tomato purée and vinegar and combine everything together.

2 Cover with a lid and simmer over your lowest heat for 2 hours. Add a little more stock if required (the mixture should be sloppy). Season with salt and pepper.

3 Preheat the oven to 180°C (350°F), Gas Mark 4.

4 Without separating the rolls, slice them horizontally and place the lower half in a baking tray or ovenproof dish lined with greaseproof paper. Mix together the butter, garlic and parsley (if using), then brush this onto the bottom half. Spoon the minced beef mixture over the rolls, then top with the cheese slices and the top half of the rolls. Brush the tops of the rolls with any remaining garlic butter.

5 Bake in the oven for 8–10 minutes, until the cheese has melted. Use the paper to lift the slider bake from the tray and bring to the dinner table to enjoy. I serve mine with oven chips and some creamy coleslaw on the side.

SLOW COOKER METHOD

1 Follow step 1 as above, making sure you use only 200 ml (⅓ pint) of stock.

2 Transfer this to your slow cooker, then cover and cook on the low setting for 4 hours. Season with salt and pepper.

3 Follow steps 3–5 as above.

Desserts and Drinks

You might be surprised at the array of desserts you can make in your slow cooker. I bet you expected slow-cooked fruit like baked apples, but no, I'm going to introduce you to sponges, puddings, cheesecakes, crème brûlées and even a few drinks you can enjoy alongside these amazing desserts.

If I'm totally honest, I was surprised at how versatile a slow cooker can be when it comes to desserts. Okay, there is the slight drawback that you can't achieve that crispy buttery crust on a pudding like a crumble, but you just have to think outside the box a little. My nutty crumble topping, spiked with maple syrup, is made separately and sprinkled over just before serving. As a bonus, this crumble is also amazing as a granola sprinkled over fruit and yogurt for breakfast.

SLOW-BAKED RHUBARB CHEESECAKE

This dessert relies on a slow cooking process, and whether you achieve that in a slow cooker or in the oven, the results will be spectacular. Rhubarb is one of my favourite ingredients and its sharpness cuts through the sweet and creamy cheesecake filling. Of course, you don't have to add the fruit – a basic baked vanilla cheesecake is a legend in its own right.

SERVES 6

Base:
100 g (3½ oz) gingernut biscuits,
  broken down to a fine crumb
  by blitzing in a food processor
  or by sealing in a ziplock bag and
  bashing with a rolling pin
40 g (1½ oz) unsalted butter, melted

Rhubarb layer:
15 g (½ oz) unsalted butter
200 g (7 oz) rhubarb, cut into 4 cm
  (1½ inch) pieces
20 g (¾ oz) golden caster sugar
1 tablespoon Amaretto liqueur
  (optional)

Filling:
3 eggs
250 g (9 oz) cream cheese
90 g (3¼ oz) caster sugar
5 tablespoons soured cream
1 teaspoon cornflour
1 teaspoon vanilla extract

30 g (1 oz) caster sugar, for
  caramelizing

CONVENTIONAL METHOD

1 Line the base and sides of a 15 cm (6 inch) springform cake tin with nonstick baking paper. Transfer the biscuit crumbs to a bowl and mix in the melted butter. Place the mixture in the lined tin. Compress it down and push some of the biscuit base up the sides of the tin to hold the rhubarb in place later on. Chill in the refrigerator for 20 minutes. Take a large piece of foil and wrap it around the base and up the sides of the tin to make a waterproof seal.
2 Preheat the oven to 160°C (325°F), Gas Mark 3.
3 Make the rhubarb filling by melting the butter in a pan, then add the remaining ingredients and cook gently for 6–7 minutes, until the rhubarb is tender but still holding its shape. Drain off any excess liquid, then leave to cool before pouring the rhubarb over the base and smoothing into an even layer.
4 Place the eggs, cream cheese, sugar, soured cream, cornflour and vanilla extract in a bowl and mix using a hand whisk until fully combined. Pour this mixture into the cake tin then sit the cake tin in a roasting tin.
5 Fill the roasting tin with boiling water until it comes two-thirds of the way up the sides of the cake tin. Bake in the oven for 45–50 minutes, until set but with a slight wobble in the centre. Leave to stand for 20 minutes before carefully removing from the springform tin and transferring to a serving plate. Place in in the refrigerator for at least 5 hours, or overnight, to chill and set completely.
6 To serve, sprinkle over the sugar and caramelize with a cook's blowtorch or under a hot grill.

SLOW COOKER METHOD

1 Follow steps 1, 3 and 4 as above.
2 Make a trivet for your slow cooker (*see* Tip on page 169), then pour in boiling water until it's 2.5 cm (1 inch) deep. Place the springform tin in the slow cooker, cover with a clean tea towel with the edges draped down the outside of the pot and then put on the lid. Pull the tea towel tight until it's taut. Cook on the low setting for 2 hours. The centre should have a slight wobble.
3 Remove from the slow cooker and leave to stand for 20 minutes before carefully removing from the springform tin and transferring to a serving plate. Place in the refrigerator for at least 5 hours, or overnight, to chill and set completely.
4 Follow step 6 as above.

RASPBERRY AND WHITE CHOCOLATE BREAD AND BUTTER PUDDING

This recipe can be used as the basis for any flavour combination – try chocolate and orange, whiskey and raisin or toffee apple – so get creative in the kitchen, because that's where the real fun begins! Serve with a scoop of vanilla ice cream and, if you want to be really bad, a dollop of rich Cornish clotted cream on top of that. I know I've called it bread and butter pudding, but since I'm using brioche it really doesn't need the extra butter.

SERVES 4

Butter, for greasing
1 brioche loaf, approx. 200 g (7 oz)
150 g (5½ oz) raspberries
40 g (1½ oz) marmalade, warmed

Custard:
250 ml (9 fl oz) double cream
200 ml (⅓ pint) milk
3 egg yolks
40 g (1½ oz) caster sugar
80 g (2¾ oz) white chocolate, broken into small pieces

To serve (optional):
Vanilla ice cream
Clotted cream

CONVENTIONAL METHOD

1 Preheat the oven to 160°C (325°F), Gas Mark 3. Grease a 25 cm x 18 cm (10 inch x 7 inch) baking dish with butter.
2 Cut the brioche into slices 1 cm (½ inch) thick, then cut each slice in half diagonally. Layer the brioche triangles in the buttered baking dish, scattering the raspberries between them as you go.
3 Make the custard by gently heating the cream and milk in a pan. Put the egg yolks and sugar in a heatproof bowl and whisk to combine, then gradually pour in the hot milk mixture, whisking as you go. Pour this back into the pan and return to a very low heat, then stir through the chocolate until it has all melted.
4 Pour the custard over the brioche and put the dish in a roasting tin. Fill the tin with boiling water until it comes two-thirds of the way up the sides of the dish, then bake in the oven for 35–40 minutes, until the custard has set and the bread is golden. After 20 minutes, brush on the warmed marmalade and return to the oven to finish baking. Serve with ice cream and clotted cream, if liked.

SLOW COOKER METHOD

1 Cut the brioche into slices 1 cm (½ inch) thick, then cut each slice in half diagonally. Butter your slow cooker pot, then layer in the brioche triangles, scattering the raspberries between the layers as you go and pushing them in between the slices.
2 Follow step 3 as above to make the custard.
3 Pour the custard over the bread, then pop on the lid and cook on the low setting for 2 hours. Before serving, brush on the warmed marmalade to glaze. Serve with ice cream and clotted cream, if liked.

SUMMER FRUIT NUT CRUMBLE

I love to take advantage of the free fruit knocking around in the summer months. As a kid we used to spend hours on end picking blackberries and going 'crabbing' or 'scrumping' for apples, as we called it in the West Country. They are memories that will last a lifetime and it's something I love doing with Indie now too, although half the battle is stopping her from eating all the fruit before we get home! The crumble mix can be stored in an airtight container for a couple of weeks if you want to make a little more than required, ready for next time.

SERVES 4

30 g (1 oz) unsalted butter, plus extra for greasing
1 large Bramley apple, peeled, cored and cut into 2.5 cm (1 inch) pieces
100 g (3½ oz) Braeburn apples, peeled, cored and cut into 2.5 cm (1 inch) pieces
100 g (3½ oz) ripe pears, peeled, cored and cut into 2.5 cm (1 inch) pieces
60 g (2¼ oz) golden caster sugar
200 g (7 oz) blackberries
Clotted cream, to serve

Crumble:
50 g (1¾ oz) rolled oats
40 g (1½ oz) crushed hazelnuts
40 g (1½ oz) flaked almonds
20 g (¾ oz) unsalted butter, melted
3 tablespoons maple syrup

CONVENTIONAL METHOD

1 Preheat the oven to 180°C (350°F), Gas Mark 4. Lightly grease a 25 cm x 18 cm (10 inch x 7 inch) baking dish with butter.
2 Melt the butter in a pan, then add the apples, pears and sugar and cook gently for around 10 minutes, until softened. Stir in the blackberries, then transfer to the buttered baking dish.
3 To make the crumble, mix the oats and nuts in a bowl, then add the melted butter and maple syrup and stir well. Top the fruit with the crumble, then bake in the oven for 20–25 minutes, until golden. Leave to cool for 5 minutes before serving with some clotted cream.

SLOW COOKER METHOD

1 Set your slow cooker to high, then pop the butter into the pot. When the butter has melted, add the apples, pears, blackberries and sugar and stir well. Pop the lid on and cook for 1 hour.
2 Pull the lid to one side so there is a decent-sized gap. This will help some of the liquid evaporate. Cook for a further hour, until the fruit is tender.
3 While the fruit is cooking, preheat the oven to 180°C (350°F), Gas Mark 4. Line a baking sheet with nonstick baking paper.
4 For the crumble, mix the oats and nuts in a bowl, then add the melted butter and maple syrup and stir well. Scatter onto the lined baking sheet and bake in the oven for 20–25 minutes, until golden. Remove from the oven and cool.
5 Portion the fruit into serving bowls, then scatter the nut crumble over the top and serve with clotted cream.

HOT TIPPLES

Picture this: it's a chilly summer evening in the garden or a frosty winter's eve sat by the fire. In either case, these comforting, spiced and gently mulled drinks are guaranteed to warm your cockles and probably make you a little tipsy too!

FESTIVE MULLED WINE

SERVES 8

2 bottles of red wine
2 large oranges, peeled and juiced
1 lemon, peeled and juiced
100 g (3½ oz) sugar (or to taste)
8 cloves
2 star anise
2 cinnamon sticks

CONVENTIONAL METHOD

1 Pour the red wine, orange and lemon juice into a large pan. Toss in the orange and lemon zest, sugar, cloves, star anise and cinnamon sticks, then cover with a lid and bring up to a simmer. Heat gently for 40 minutes so the spices can infuse the wine. Ladle into mugs or glasses to serve.

SLOW COOKER METHOD

1 Pour all the ingredients into your slow cooker, including the orange and lemon zest. Cover with a lid and leave to mull on the medium setting for at least 1 hour. Before serving, give it a good stir and adjust with sugar to taste, then ladle into mugs or glasses.

MULLED WEST COUNTRY CIDER

SERVES 8

2 litres (3½ pints) good-quality
   dry West Country cider
1 large orange
8 cloves
1 thumb-sized piece of fresh root
   ginger, sliced
2 star anise
2 cinnamon sticks
3–4 tablespoons sugar (or to taste)

CONVENTIONAL METHOD

1 Pour the cider into a large pan. Stud the orange with the cloves, then cut it in half and add to the cider along with the ginger, star anise, cinnamon sticks and sugar. Cover with a lid and bring up to a simmer. Heat gently for 40 minutes so the spices can infuse the cider. Ladle into mugs or glasses to serve.

SLOW COOKER METHOD

1 Pour the cider into your slow cooker. Stud the orange with the cloves, then cut it in half and add to the cider along with the ginger, star anise, cinnamon sticks and sugar. Cover with a lid and leave to mull on the medium setting for at least 1 hour. Before serving, give it a good stir and adjust with sugar to taste, then ladle into mugs or glasses.

GINGERBREAD SPICED HOT CHOCOLATE

When the dark nights and chilly winter evenings creep in, it's the perfect excuse to bust out the antidote to the frosty weather: a steaming mug of hot chocolate. I still remember schooldays running in from the playground after kicking a football around at –2°C to be welcomed by a jug of the magical elixir complete with a skin on top. Adults and kids alike will love this one. Top with a few mini marshmallows for an extra treat.

SERVES 6

800 ml (28 fl oz) milk

1 x 400 g (14 oz) can of sweetened
    condensed milk

1 teaspoon ground ginger

½ teaspoon ground cinnamon

Small grating of nutmeg

150 g (5½ oz) dark chocolate, at least
    70 per cent cocoa solids, broken
    into small chunks

Caster sugar, to taste

Mini marshmallows, to serve

CONVENTIONAL METHOD

1 Heat the milk and condensed milk in a pot along with the spices until boiling. Remove from the heat and add the chocolate, whisking as you go until it has all melted. Add the sugar a little at a time until it's sweet enough. Keep warm until ready to serve.

2 Ladle into mugs and add a handful of mini marshmallows on top. You can melt them a little with a chef's blowtorch if you like.

SLOW COOKER METHOD

1 Put the milk, condensed milk and spices into your slow cooker. Cover and cook on the high setting for 1 hour, then add the chocolate and stir until it has all melted. Add the sugar a little at a time until it's sweet enough. Turn to the warm setting and let it tick over until you're ready to serve.

2 Follow step 2 as above.

SELF-SAUCING CHOCOLATE ORANGE PUDDING

As a kid I thought this was the best thing ever – I genuinely never thought I would taste anything better as long as I lived. When I was let in on the secret recipe, I couldn't believe how simple it was. Give this one a try, I guarantee the family will love it.

SERVES 6

115 g (4 oz) unsalted butter, softened,
  plus extra for greasing
115 g (4 oz) caster sugar
2 eggs, beaten
1 teaspoon vanilla extract
85 g (3 oz) self-raising flour
30 g (1 oz) cocoa powder
Pinch of salt
2 tablespoons milk
50 g (1¾ oz) mini marshmallows

Sauce:
180 g (6¼ oz) soft brown sugar
60 g (2¼ oz) cocoa powder
300 ml (½ pint) boiling water
Juice and finely grated zest of 1 orange

CONVENTIONAL METHOD

1 Preheat the oven to 180°C (350°F), Gas Mark 4. Grease a 25 cm x 18 cm (10 inch x 7 inch) baking dish with butter.
2 Cream the butter and sugar together in a large bowl, then beat in the eggs and vanilla extract. Sift in the flour, cocoa and salt, then gently fold through until combined and add the milk – you should have a medium-soft consistency. Fold through the marshmallows, then spoon into the well-buttered baking dish.
3 Combine all the sauce ingredients and stir well, then carefully pour it over the sponge mixture. Bake in the oven for 40–45 minutes, until the sponge has risen and a skewer inserted into the centre comes out clean.

SLOW COOKER METHOD

1 Grease the slow cooker pot with butter.
2 Follow step 2 as above, but spoon into the slow cooker.
3 Combine all the sauce ingredients and stir well, then carefully pour it over the sponge mixture. Cover and cook on the high setting for 2 hours. Don't be tempted to open the slow cooker while it's cooking!

VANILLA POACHED PEARS

I cooked a version of this during my *MasterChef* quarterfinal. Gregg Wallace declared it a thing of beauty and who am I to argue? These pears are sweet, rich and delicious. An acidic Greek yogurt is my preferred accompaniment, but if you fancy mixing it up, a drizzle of hot chocolate sauce (like the one used in the Chocolate Banana Croissant Pudding on page 215) is a real treat.

SERVES 4

250 ml (9 fl oz) sweet dessert wine

250 ml (9 fl oz) boiling water

40 g (1½ oz) caster sugar

Zest of ½ lemon

Small squeeze of lemon juice

8 star anise

1 vanilla pod, split in half lengthways
    and seeds scraped out

2 large pears, peeled and halved

To serve:

Greek yogurt

50 g (1¾ oz) amaretti biscuits,
    crushed

CONVENTIONAL METHOD

1 Pour the wine and water into a pan, then add the sugar, lemon zest and juice, star anise and the vanilla seeds and pod. Bring up to the boil and stir until the sugar has dissolved.

2 Remove the cores from the pears with a melon baller or metal teaspoon, then pop the pears into the pan, cover with a lid and simmer gently for 20–25 minutes, until they are tender.

3 Lift the pears from the pan and reduce the poaching liquid until syrupy.

4 Press a star anise into the hollowed-out core of each pear half. Serve the pears with a drizzle of the syrup, some Greek yogurt and a sprinkling of the crushed amaretti biscuits.

SLOW COOKER METHOD

1 Pour the wine and water into the slow cooker, then add the sugar, lemon zest and juice, star anise and the vanilla seeds and pod. Stir until the sugar has dissolved.

2 Remove the cores from the pears with a melon baller or metal teaspoon, then pop them into the slow cooker. Cover and cook on the low setting for 2 hours, until the pears are tender.

3 Transfer some of the poaching liquid to a pan and reduce until syrupy.

4 Follow step 4 as above.

STICKY TOFFEE PUDDING

What can I say about this pudding? If I see this dessert on a menu when eating out, it's as good as ordered. When cooking at home I like to add a good pinch of salt to the toffee sauce. I asked friends round when testing this recipe and they couldn't believe it had been made in a slow cooker. I was buzzing because this just shows the diversity of dishes that can be created.

SERVES 4–6

180 g (6¼ oz) Medjool dates, pitted
 and chopped
150 ml (¼ pint) boiling water
90 g (3¼ oz) unsalted butter,
 softened, plus extra for greasing
140 g (5 oz) dark muscovado sugar
2 eggs
40 g (1½ oz) black treacle
175 g (6 oz) self-raising flour
1 teaspoon bicarbonate of soda
Clotted cream, to serve

Toffee sauce:
100 g (3½ oz) unsalted butter
100 g (3½ oz) dark muscovado sugar
150 ml (¼ pint) double cream
Pinch of salt

CONVENTIONAL METHOD

1 Soak the dates in the boiling water for 30 minutes, then use the back of a fork to break them down.
2 Preheat the oven to 170°C (340°F), Gas Mark 3. Grease a 25 cm x 18 cm (10 inch x 7 inch) baking dish with butter.
3 While the dates are soaking, beat the butter and sugar until light and fluffy, then beat in the eggs one at a time. Whisk through the treacle, then sift in the flour and bicarbonate of soda and mix to combine.
4 Spoon the sponge batter into the buttered baking dish and bake in the oven for 50–55 minutes, until a skewer inserted into the centre comes out clean.
5 To make the toffee sauce, pop the butter, sugar, cream and a pinch of salt into a pan and heat gently until the sugar dissolves. Bring to a boil, then reduce the heat and simmer for 2–3 minutes, until thickened.
6 Cut the sponge into squares and serve with a good helping of the warm toffee sauce and a dollop of clotted cream.

SLOW COOKER METHOD

1 Follow steps 1 and 3 as above.
2 Grease your slow cooker pot with butter, then spoon in the sponge batter. Pop the lid on and cook on the high setting for 1 hour 45 minutes. Remove the lid and turn off the power, then leave to stand for 10 minutes before serving.
3 Follow steps 5–6.

CHOCOLATE AND TOFFEE S'MORES FONDUE

For those times when you want to offer something sweet to friends and family but also want something simple to make, this is the recipe you're looking for. My chocolate and toffee s'mores fondue was inspired by the sweet American snack that's usually enjoyed around a campfire: chocolate and melted marshmallow sandwiched between two biscuits or, if you can get hold of them, the all-American Graham crackers.

SERVES 8–10

1 x 400 g (14 oz) can of evaporated milk
200 g (7 oz) dark chocolate, at least 70 per cent cocoa solids, broken into pieces
80 g (2¾ oz) chewy toffees (I like Werther's)
½ teaspoon sea salt flakes (or to taste)
20 large marshmallows
Graham crackers, biscuits and fruit, to serve

CONVENTIONAL METHOD

1 Place the evaporated milk, chocolate and toffees in a heatproof bowl set over a pan of barely simmering water, making sure the water doesn't touch the bottom of the bowl. Stir until all the ingredients have melted and the chocolate fondue is silky-smooth. Add the salt to taste.

2 Decant into a serving pot, top with the marshmallows and toast with a chef's blowtorch until they are golden. Serve with Graham crackers, biscuits and fruit for dipping.

SLOW COOKER METHOD

1 Pop the evaporated milk, chocolate and toffees into your slow cooker and cook on the low setting, uncovered, for 1 hour. Stir occasionally until all the ingredients have melted.

2 Top with the marshmallows and toast with a chef's blowtorch until they are golden. Either serve immediately or switch the slow cooker to the warm setting until needed. Serve with Graham crackers, biscuits and fruit for dipping.

MOLTEN SALTED CARAMEL FONDANTS

My neighbour Gary asked me to come up with a lovely dessert as an anniversary surprise for his wife Kate and this was the result. While testing the recipes for this book, curiosity got the better of me and I thought, 'Slow cooker fondants aren't a thing, are they?' Well, I can categorically say they are not – they just didn't work, no matter how hard I tried – but these were so good I know you'll love them anyway!

SERVES 6

150 g (5½ oz) salted caramel
  (shop-bought is fine)
200 g (7 oz) unsalted butter,
  plus extra for greasing
200 g (7 oz) dark chocolate, at
  least 70 per cent cocoa solids
190 g (6¾ oz) caster sugar
4 egg yolks
2 large eggs
40 g (1½ oz) plain flour
20 g (¾ oz) cocoa powder, plus
  extra for dusting the ramekins
1 teaspoon baking powder
Small pinch of salt

CONVENTIONAL METHOD

1 Weigh out 4 x 25 g (1 oz) portions of salted caramel, then twist up each portion in clingfilm to form a ball. Pop into the freezer for 2 hours.
2 Preheat the oven to 200°C (400°F), Gas Mark 6.
3 Melt the butter and chocolate in a heatproof bowl placed over a pan of lightly simmering water, making sure the water doesn't touch the bottom of the bowl. Set aside to cool slightly.
4 Meanwhile, whisk the sugar, egg yolks and whole eggs for a couple of minutes, until pale and fluffy, then mix through the melted chocolate. Sift in the flour, cocoa and baking powder and fold in along with a small pinch of salt.
5 Butter 6 nonstick ramekins or dariole moulds (I used moulds with a 7.5cm, 3 inch, diameter and 5cm, 2 inch, height), then dust with cocoa powder, tapping out the excess. Fill the ramekins with the fondant mixture halfway, then unwrap the frozen salted caramel and place a ball in the centre of each ramekin. Top with more of the fondant mix until the filling sits 1 cm (½ inch) below the rim of the ramekin, then smooth it flat.
6 Place the ramekins or moulds on a baking tray and bake in the oven for 13 minutes. Remove from the oven and leave to stand for 1 minute before turning out onto a plate to serve.

SLOW COOKER METHOD

1 Don't bother, they don't work!

POPCORN CRÈME BRÛLÉE

A beautifully set crème brûlée is a glorious thing – creamy custard with a crisp, crunchy topping that adds texture and bitterness. Regardless of which method you use to caramelize the top of your crème brûlée, the recipe relies on gentle slow cooking, so whether you cook it in your oven or in your slow cooker, this is guaranteed to be a winner. You can infuse lots of different flavours into your custard, so why not try adding a few sprigs of lemon thyme, a squeeze of lemon or orange juice or the classic vanilla pod?

SERVES 4

400 ml (14 fl oz) double cream
50 ml (2 fl oz) milk
100 g (3½ oz) toffee popcorn
5 egg yolks
50 g (1¾ oz) caster sugar
4 teaspoons golden caster sugar

CONVENTIONAL METHOD

1 Bring the cream and milk to a simmer along with the popcorn. Turn off the heat and leave to infuse for 10 minutes, then strain to remove the popcorn.
2 Preheat the oven to 150°C (300°F), Gas Mark 2.
3 Beat the egg yolks and sugar together, then pour in the popcorn-flavoured cream mixture, whisking as you go.
4 Pour the custard into 4 ramekins, then place the ramekins in a roasting tin. Fill the tin with boiling water until it reaches halfway up the sides of the ramekins. Bake in the oven for 30–40 minutes, until just set. Leave to cool before chilling in the refrigerator for at least 4 hours until ready to serve.
5 Sprinkle each set cream with 1 teaspoon of golden caster sugar, then caramelize with a chef's blowtorch or under a very hot grill.

SLOW COOKER METHOD

1 Follow steps 1 and 3 as above.
2 Pour the custard into 4 ramekins, then stand the ramekins on top of a trivet inside of your slow cooker. Pour in boiling water until it comes one-third of the way up the sides of the ramekins. Put on the lid and cook on the low setting for 2 hours.
3 Remove the ramekins from the slow cooker and leave to cool before chilling in the refrigerator for at least 4 hours until ready to serve.
4 Follow step 5 as above.

CHOCOLATE BANANA CROISSANT PUDDING

There are some flavour combinations that just click, and for me, chocolate and banana fall into that category. Using pain au chocolat or chocolate croissants adds a whole new level of richness, but feel free to use plain croissants, brioche or even a stale white loaf you have knocking around in the cupboard.

SERVES 4–6

Butter, for greasing
8 chocolate croissants, cut in half
   horizontally
Icing sugar, for dusting

Custard:
2 ripe bananas, sliced
250 ml (9 fl oz) milk
300 ml (½ pint) double cream
4 egg yolks
40 g (1½ oz) golden caster sugar

Hot chocolate sauce:
125 g (4½ oz) golden caster sugar
125 ml (4 fl oz) water
30 g (1 oz) dark chocolate, at least
   70 per cent cocoa solids, chopped
30 g (1 oz) cocoa powder

CONVENTIONAL METHOD

1 Preheat the oven to 160°C (325°F), Gas Mark 3. Grease a 33 cm x 25 cm (13 inch x 10 inch) baking dish with butter.
2 Make the custard by first blitzing the bananas and milk in a mini blender. Transfer this to a pan with the cream and heat gently to a simmer. Whisk together the egg yolks and sugar in a heatproof bowl, then slowly whisk in the heated cream mixture, beating as you go.
3 Place the halved croissants in the buttered baking dish. Pour the custard over the croissants and set the dish in a roasting tin. Fill the tin with boiling water until it comes two-thirds of the way up the sides of the dish, then bake in the oven for 35–40 minutes, until the custard has set and the croissants are golden.
4 To make the hot chocolate sauce, bring the sugar and water to the boil in a pan, then add the chocolate and cocoa powder and stir until fully incorporated. Reduce to a medium to high heat and simmer until thickened slightly. Remove from the heat and keep warm.
5 To serve, dust the pudding with icing sugar and caramelize it with a chef's blowtorch if you have one. Enjoy with a drizzle of the chocolate sauce.

SLOW COOKER METHOD

1 Grease your slow cooker pot with butter, then add the halved croissants.
2 Follow step 2 as above to make the custard, then pour this over the croissants. Cover with the lid and cook on the low setting for 2 hours.
3 Follow steps 4–5 as above.

Index

A

achiote paste 115
alcohol:
    Amaretto 194
    bourbon 154
    brandy 155
    cider, *see main entry*
    lager 109, 147
    mulled 200
    scrumpy 170
    stout 108
    vodka 160
    wine, *see main entry*
allspice 43, 115
almonds 52, 151, 198
Amaretto 194
Angela's Welsh Lamb Cawl 86
annatto seeds 115
apple juice 173
apple sauce 170
apples 52, 198
apricots 63, 140
avocados 56, 115

B

baby spinach 151
bacon 30, 40, 82, 98, 133 (*see also* lardons)
baked beans 150
bakes 40–1
baking powder 213
bananas 215
bánh mì 87
Barbecue Pulled Pork 83, *84–5*
Barbecue Sauce 82
barbecue sauce 27, 154
basil 25, 64, 160
Béchamel Sauce 180
beef:
    brisket 128
    chuck 108
    consommé 128, 148
    curry 120–1
    marrowbone 127
    minced 40, 187
    pie 153
    pulled 42
    ragù 30
    rendang 80
    ribs 112
    shin 32, 127
    short ribs 112
    skirt 30, 42, 80, 108, 120, 153
    stock 30, 32, 40, 42, 80, 108, 116, 120, 127, 133, 153, 176, 187
    suet 140
    tips for cooking 127
Beef Bourguignon 176–7
Beef Brisket French Dip Rolls 128
Beef Pantry Pie *152*, 153
Beef Shin Osso Bucco *126*, 127
belly pork 87, 170
berry fruits 195, 198
bicarbonate of soda 208
bird's-eye chillies 132
biscuits:
    amaretti 205
    gingernut 194
    savoury 210
black beans 56
blackberries 198
Blue Cheese and Bacon Slaw 186
bouillabaisse 35
bouquet garni 173
bourbon 154
Bourbon Barbecue Chicken Enchiladas 154
bourguignon 176–7
Braised Faggots in Rich Cider Gravy *102*, 103
brandy 155
Brazilian Fish Stew 60–1
bread-and-butter pudding 195
breadcrumbs 122, 133, 150
Breakfast Shakshuka 53, *54–5*
breyani 68–9
Brining Liquid 168

brioche 38, 195
brisket 128
broccoli 99, 103
Buffalo Pulled Chicken with Blue Cheese and Bacon Slaw 186
Buffalo sauce 186
butter beans 73
butternut squash 63

C

cabbage 34, 86, 181, 186
cacao, *see* cocoa
cacciatore 94
cannellini beans 56, 64, 124
Caprese Chicken Melt *24*, 25
caramel:
    fondants 213
    salted 213
cardamom 120, 132, 179
Caribbean Goat Curry 123
Caribbean Lamb Curry 43, *44–5*
Carrot and Onion Sambal 122
carrots 30, 40, 64, 72, 86, 87, 99, 122, 127, 133, 140, 142, 170, 173, 176
cashew nuts 90
casseroles:
    chicken 95
    sausage 150
cassoulet 124–5
cauliflower 129
cavolo nero 170
cawl 86
celery 30, 37, 64, 73, 108, 127, 133, 142, 170
champ 95
Char Sui Shredded Beef 42
cheeks:
    ox 116
    pig 124
Cheese Fondue with Garlic Tear 'n' Share Loaf 166–7
cheesecakes 194
cheeses:
    blue 148, 186

Thank you

I feel very privileged to have been given the opportunity to write my third cookbook. But of course it's not all down to me – without the help of many, many people, this simply would not have been possible, so here goes (and please forgive me if I've missed anyone out).

The team at Octopus has been amazing! Sarah Reece, you are a star. Without you championing this book, it wouldn't have happened. I was very blessed to have such a magnificent team bringing this book to life: Polly, Jaz, Ria, Cynthia and my fabulous home ec, Sara Lewis. Thank you so much, guys.

It feels like every time I get to write my thank yous, I get deep thinking about all the people who have helped, supported and encouraged me along my journey. This time, my biggest fan, my Uncle Steve – my godfather, birthday partner and someone I idolized – won't be here to share in my success. This book is dedicated to you and I'll never forget what you did for me.

Thank you to Jan, Borra, Louise and Tang at Deborah McKenna Ltd for looking after me all these years. We've been together a long time and I hope we have many more successful years to come.

Lizzy, it must have been extremely hard work for you to have been chief tester while I was writing this book. I love that you enjoy my food. You have been an incredible support to me over the last year, always there for me when I've needed you most. I think you are amazing.

Now to my long-suffering family. You keep going even though I bore you to tears asking you to share my cooking posts and pictures, but it's never too much for any of you. I hope I make you proud. A special mention to Lou – even though you don't have any of my cookbooks and probably won't see this one either, thanks for your support and the incredible job you do raising my baby girl, even when I'm away working for days at a time. You're always my best mate.

Finally, to my inspiration, my baby girl Indie-Roux. My life changed when I had you. I love you so much and every day I strive to be a better dad to you. I'll also keep embarrassing you by dancing, singing and telling bad jokes and I'll continue to annoy you by constantly taking pictures of you. One day you will realize that I do this to document our lives together and capture the happiness you bring into my life. Watching you grow into a beautiful young woman makes me so proud.